Isaiah and Me

© Copyright Joy Simons
Published by Glorybound Publishing
SAN 256-4564
10 9 8 7 6 5 4 3 2 1
Printed in the United States of America
ISBN 9781699932094
Copyright data is available on file.
Simons, Joy, 1957-
        Isaiah and Me/Joy Simons
        Includes biographical reference.
1. Inspirational   2. Biography
I. Title

www.gloryboundpublishing.com
www.psalm42-7.net

The photo used on the cover by permission is from Lake Powell looking over Bullfrog Basin. By Sheri Hauser. 2012.

Unless otherwise marked, the Bible used for all the Isaiah passages is The Interlinear Hebrew-Greek-English Bible, by Jay P. Green, Sr and published by Hendrickson Publishers. It is painstakingly translated, and the corresponding Strong's Concordance number is added above each word. His work made mine easier and opened bigger doors of understanding. I encourage those of you interested in Bible research to find a set.

Bible translations included in this text are from "The Passion Translation" (TPT) and "The Message Bible" (MSG).

Unless otherwise marked, all of the additional New Testament passages are quoted from New King James Version (NKJV).

Dedication

This book is dedicated to
the bride of Christ. May we find our
identity in Him and our love for each other.

Many Thanks

Many thanks to friends who helped me in this process: Ray and Debry Taylor, my sister – Allie Weathersby, Leah Wilcock and Linda Killman. Your insights and editing of the manuscript helped to make this book so much better. I value the depth of your relationship with Christ and your honesty with me.

Thank you also to the readers of my blog: Psalm42-7.net. The work for this book started with your responses to my commentary. Your support has been a source of strength for me.

Special thanks to Chris Canning, who continues to pray with me through thick and thin. You are a testimony of God's steadfastness. I will forever be grateful for your friendship.

The Gate of the Year

And I said to the man who stood at the gate of
the year,
"Give me a light that I may tread safely into
the unknown."
And he replied,
"Go out into the darkness and put your hand
into the Hand of God.
That shall be to you better than light and safer
than a known way."
So I went forth, and finding the Hand of God,
trod gladly into the night.
And He led me towards the hills and the
breaking day in the lone East.

Minnie Louise Haskins

ISAIAH AND ME

By
Joy Simons

Glorybound Publishing
Camp Verde, Arizona
Released 2019

Letter from the Author

About 4 ½ years ago, the Lord asked me to read Isaiah. When I finished, He said, "Read it again." I lost count of the times I have read it, but out of that assignment came a complete commentary on Isaiah's relevance to us today. (That is found on my website: psalm42-7.net).

Though it took me years to complete, I was astounded that every word Isaiah wrote 2700 years ago had deep meaning to the Church and to us! When the commentary was complete, God directed me to write this book.

I was confused. "I just finished the whole thing. Do You want me just to put them all together?" The answer was to find the common thread through Isaiah and write about that. So, I dove back in to reread the book, this time comfortable with the familiarity of his words.

Then I realized that this book is the journey of growing faith in Isaiah. Many scholars believe that Isaiah was written by 2 or 3 people and compiled together into one book. But when you realize the changes Isaiah went through in his walk with God, the changes that are right there on the page, it becomes clear that this one man wrote it all and we are watching his relationship with God grow from glory to glory.

Isaiah's journey is also my journey and your journey. I wove my story inside Isaiah's to show how all of us are like him, walking and stumbling into intimacy with Jesus.

Isaiah concludes with ten glorious chapters about the Church, and since the Church is God's people, this also is about our journey to God. Our journey together as the bride of Christ is more exciting than our own.

I hope you will see yourself rising closer to God as you read this. This book isn't just my story or Isaiah's story; it is the common threads of all our lives. It is reaching for something so much better than ourselves. It is hearing His voice. It is finding a love that satisfies all our needs and heals our souls. Join me in this journey.

ISAIAH AND ME

Introduction

"We shall not cease from exploration, and the end of all our exploring will be to arrive where we started and know the place for the first time." T S Elliot

All of us have a start when we begin to learn who we are and what life is like. Then we have a beginning when we start to unlearn everything we know in the face of the truth of God.

This is a book about Isaiah's journey unlearning religion as he knew it and meeting God. This is also the story of my "unlearning" journey. But, most important, it's about you and me together in unity with Jesus and Holy Spirit, creating the holy Church of God.

Isaiah, whether he knew it or not, wrote about Jesus; His birth, His life, His crucifixion, and His resurrection. His book is a commentary of Jesus' ministry, sometimes showing us incredible details about intimate moments. While Isaiah was addressing the sins of Israel and the world, speaking words of comfort to his people, and advising kings, God was using the same words to tell us all about His Son and what He would (and does) do.

Our journey of faith, as told in the book of Isaiah, begins at the awakening of our spirits to the reality of God. The path to deep intimacy with Him leads to ultimate joy; the pain of repentance wrapped in the unending and unstoppable love of our Creator that overcomes our hurts and floods us with Himself.

He is forever calling to us, wooing us into His heart. His hand stretched out is for us to find as we grope through life looking for meaning. We move cautiously through the darkness searching for light, and He travels along-side us waiting for our yieldedness to give Him entrance.

This journey has many facets. I call them facets because they can all be seen individually, but the beauty of the gem is not appreciated until they are seen as a whole. No matter the order, our facets of learning: rules, experience, love, repentance, intimacy, change, all have their benchmark moments. They can happen together, separately, or over and over again in ever-deepening levels. They are a continuous work in our lives as we move from glory to glory.

> "The moment one turns to the Lord with an open heart, the veil [of understanding] is lifted and they see. . .We can all draw close to Him with the veil removed from our faces. And with no veil we all become like mirrors who brightly reflect the glory of the Lord Jesus. We are being transfigured into His very image as we move from one brighter level of glory to another. And this glorious transfiguration comes from the Lord." (2 Corinthians 3:16-18, TPT)

God's journey to us is our journey to Him.

Awakening to His presence

> "Awake, you who sleep. Arise from the dead, and Christ will give you light." (Ephesians 5:14)

All of us are searching for God. We want that "thing" that will set us up and give us the security and happiness that we can carry for the rest of our lives. We invest ourselves in money markets, marriages, religions, health kicks, mysticism, horoscopes, whatever - because we need to feel in control, on top of things. Yet, when we do get control, it is not the easy street we thought it would be.

What we want is a version of God that is all hearts and flowers – a being who is in control and works the world to accommodate our lives. What we _need_ is a relationship with God. Our ultimate happiness and peace is within this relationship as it grows into a life of faith and trust. When we find Him, some of His goodness we can access right away. Some takes a little more time, but all of it, all of Him, is what we can have.

As we grow in faith and love, we find this relationship blesses everything we do. As we move from glory to glory, deeper and deeper into love, we are changed into the person we hoped we would be. We are given the life we only wished for. It doesn't look like what we thought it would, but it is everything we ever wanted.

This journey is not for just the few. The age of "special men and women" is past. Here is a highway made straight for *all* believers to come.

> They shall see the glory of the Lord, the excellency of our God. Strengthen the weak hands, and make firm the feeble knees. Say to those who are fearful-hearted; "Be strong, do not fear! Behold, your God will come. . . and save you." Then the eyes of the blind shall be opened, and the ears of the deaf shall be unstopped. Then the lame shall leap like a deer, and the tongue of the dumb sing. . . A highway shall be there, and a road, and it shall be called the Highway of Holiness. . . Whoever walks the road, although a fool, shall not go astray. No lion shall be there, nor shall any ravenous beast go up on it; it shall not be found there. But the redeemed shall walk there, and the ransomed of the Lord shall return, and come to Zion with singing, with everlasting joy on their heads. They shall obtain joy and gladness, and sorrow and sighing shall flee away. (Isaiah 35:2-10)

It doesn't matter where you are in your faith, whatever measure of faith you have qualifies you to walk the Highway of Holiness and every step you take brings you closer to God. This is a wonderful Jesus-Holy Spirit-God Being who loves us and desires good for us. This is an incredible Trinity that makes a way where there is no way and gently opens us to a love that strengthens, saves, heals, protects, and gives joy unbounded.

How do we find this wonderful highway? We search for God and He brings us to it. But in that search, we must walk through our "stuff." Our hearts are full of wants and needs. Without God, the futility of hopes and dreams not possible to attain causes us to sink into "facing reality." Our hearts are broken, walled up to prevent us from living in constant pain.

All this emptiness and unfulfilled desire leads us to any mountain-top experience that moves us into the frenzy of corporate joy. We search for groups or concepts that carry us out of ourselves into emotion, intellect, or ritual. Laws of behavior become our savior. The next manufactured high is a spiritual experience. The group's agreement to give or get from each other is our moral compass.

God calls us to walk away from everything we know, all that we've learned. Where we feel at home is only protecting our own defenses, built from our limited understanding of the world and our fears in it - a very weak place to be. Change is difficult. Radical change is frightening. We become like turtles, hunkering down into our shells and ignoring the opportunity for Holy intimacy. We may feel secure deep inside the shell we've built around ourselves, but one strong hammer to the back and our shells are gone and we are entirely at the mercy of our surroundings.

If we emerge from our shells seeking God, He will lead us onto the path of joy He's created for us. For me that was a long journey that begins here.

PART 1

**Our Personal Journey of Faith
Isaiah, Me and You**

God will find us;
Even hell is not too far

"Who shall separate us from the love of Christ? Shall tribulation or distress or persecution, or famine, or nakedness, or peril, or sword?" (Romans 8:35)

Cutting through the darkness to see the light of God can be very difficult. He's always there, but my blindness can be extreme, and He had to work very hard with in the beginning.

In my childhood, I was clinically depressed. My sister, brother, and I lived in a home where love was scarce and not to be trusted. We learned to survive on our own, isolated even from each other; children with only a childish understanding to fight the world. I had no idea what love was or even how to feel emotions in a healthy way.

My parents loved us, but my mother was a hard woman. She was stressed, locked in a marriage she didn't want. Divorce in the '50s and '60s was not an option for a respectable woman, and mom's coping skills were minimal. The opinions of other people were very important to her. So, in public, she was a loving mother, but behind the closed doors of our home, we learned to stay out of her way. Having children was an obligation that society demanded, but for her, we were a burden she resented, and she made it clear that our company was not something she desired.

My father escaped into work and, although he was always home for supper, he would leave again for a choir rehearsal or a meeting. There was always something keeping him out of the house, and we learned that a father's love existed in the distance, experienced in a few fleeting moments; always desired, but never fulfilled.

We three "happy-go-lucky kids" were discouraged from playing together because it was too noisy. Mom was always working on something and, since dad was hardly home, she reigned in our house. We lived a life of stony isolation, learning from rejection that we were undeserving of affection, and emotional punishment was the only attention we could receive. Until adulthood, we never played together, never talked, and shared our lives with each other. We were just occupants living in the same house; each in our own rooms and divorced from a relationship.

In this world, compliments from others seemed insincere and meaningless. They were an obligation to be displayed for public approval, but not heartfelt. The "truth" was always there, "If we weren't in public, they wouldn't be saying these things. They may like what you did, but they don't really like you. They don't really know you. Their appreciation is worthless." Of-course these are lies, but I was a child who knew only isolation and rejection. Genuine affection and appreciation were so foreign to me; I couldn't accept them as real.

On top of all that warmth and security, I am a seer. Always have been. "Seeing" things that are not of this world can be exciting if you understand what's happening, but when I was a young child, I didn't understand anything I was "seeing." Angels, demons, they all were the same in my mind; frightening things not of this earth. I had an almost paralyzing fear of the dark (that's when the things that go bump in the night began to move), and always felt a presence near me; sometimes good, sometimes bad. I thought I was on the edge of going crazy, so I never told anyone. My immature mind just decided it was up to me to hold on to sanity, and very early, I began to build psychological defenses to "protect" myself. My silent determination not to let anything hurt me was mistaken for quiet maturity, and people around me assumed I was more than I was.

Music was a sanctuary from all this craziness. I have always been able to sing and have a talent for things musical. It was the one thing dad and I shared, and I clung to it. Performing pleased him, so I threw myself into being the best performer I could be. When I was singing, my dad and other people paid attention to me. So, I gathered up those affirming moments and thought, "Maybe I'm not so bad after all."

And I did have one great friend, Barbara. We grew up together, and I shared almost everything with her. We were inseparable; went to the same small school, so we were in class together all day; went to the same Church so we saw each other every Sunday and once a week for children's choir rehearsal. When we weren't together, we were on the phone. In the time of party-lines and one phone families, this was a war I gladly fought every day.

The summer I was eleven, she was on a plane coming home from visiting her grandmother. The plane hit some fog and crashed into the side of a mountain, killing everyone on board. Although my parents knew this, they decided not to tell me. I learned from another child who had no idea how to break news like this. I didn't believe her until I tore the paper out of my father's hands, and there was the obituary. I went into shock. I have no memory of the next few days. I'm told I sat in my room and cried. My parents decided it was best that I be left alone, even they didn't come in to console me. I dealt with this grief in solitude with all the skill an 11-year-old has to process horrific things. I emerged damaged beyond belief.

At 13, I accepted Christ into my life. You would think that would be miraculous for me, but my mind was clouded by unmet needs and, although I'll never forget that beautiful moment, my needs still drove my life. Jesus was there (which was better than the darkness), but there was no guidance for living afterward. Nothing changed because I was not willing to.

Barbara's death clung to me for years. I was afraid to open myself up to close friendship again, the opposite sex opened up possibilities. When I was found attractive by a boy, there was validation. I was no longer the over-looked child who was in the way, but the center of his attention and desire. Being the most important person in the world made me happy. I didn't realize this wasn't love. I really couldn't feel that or return that. I just loved *being* loved and believed the lie that these feelings were real. Boys were walking me home from school, watching me in class, hanging out with me after school – this was heady stuff!

I always wondered why none of these boys asked me out until my brother confessed he used to threaten to beat them up if they tried anything with me. He was very protective. My sister dealt with all of this by shutting down. My brother was violent. I was sarcastic and verbally abusive sometimes. I think my brother and I might have been bullies, but we didn't see it through all of this. If we did that, please forgive. The good news – we don't do it anymore.

After a while I met MaryPaul. She and I lived near each other and went to the same Junior High and High School. We walked to and from school together (about 2 miles so we had time to talk), stayed at her house, snuck out at night, did pranks around the neighborhood, all the stuff young kids are supposed to get in trouble for. She kept me stable and was a support.

I continued to attend Church and get good grades as a good girl should. I knew this was acting, but behavior was the important thing after all. Follow the rules so that people thought you were a good person and anything else you did was excusable.

But this was not to last. MaryPaul's father was military, and so, after a few years, they moved across the country, and we lost touch. I was once again alone, and this time I was done with being vulnerable for good. A solitary life was very attractive and safe.

Eventually, a boy came along who truly loved me. We dated through the rest of high school and planned to get married. All the attention I missed was manifested in him. We clung together; he because he genuinely loved me; I because I genuinely needed love and I soaked him dry. Being an "emotional vampire" was not a conscious choice, but there it was.

When I was 15, we had sex for the first time. It was a traumatic moment for me; sex was not something I was ready for. This was vulnerability on a scale I had never dreamed of, and, after I finished sobbing, the fear of openness moved into determination to never be that vulnerable again. Now, this was in a dilemma. In my mind, the sex could not stop, or our relationship would be over, and that would crush me. I needed him to love me.

But I <u>could</u> remove my emotional involvement in the process. If I made sex just an act and not an expression of love, I just might be able to keep going. If I didn't let my heart get involved with what my body was doing, I would be alright. Sex became "self-medication." When we had sex, he was totally focused on me and us, and I was totally focused on him focusing on me. I began to think that this was the ultimate tool for real happiness.

We were both on our way to college, so the plan was to graduate from our respective schools and then start our lives together. For 2 ½ years, we had seemed devoted to each other, always together. The last 18 months we were in a long-distance relationship, he at his school and me at mine; always a few hundred miles apart. He kept me on the monogamous straight and narrow, but I wouldn't last in a long-distance relationship.

My Senior year in high school was his first year of college. My routine of class, Church, and so on kept me together until the weekends and vacations he came home. But after graduation, life got a lot more complicated.

When I got to college, there was no foundation in me to sustain my "good" life. My fiancé couldn't "feed" me with love if he wasn't there and I began to break under the pressure of study and loneliness. Alcohol introduced himself to me. I had no way to process life with mind-numbing substances so easily accessible. I began to swim into the deep end of a dangerous pool.

Then, came along a boy at my school who liked me. I couldn't resist his attentions, so close and immediate, so I broke off my engagement to dive into this new relationship. It was all so selfish and ugly, broken hearts strewn everywhere. Shame followed me for many years.

This boy was in music school with me and could give me love every day. He led me deeper into the wonderful world of parties, sex, drugs, and alcohol. We finally lived together for a while. We were getting married eventually, so what was the difference? I met his parents. Things were going well, but then he grew tired of me. Not wanting to "lose me," he suggested we spend some time seeing other people and then eventually get back together. What could I say?

Not wanting to commit to anyone else, but not having a committed relationship, I wandered into the world of promiscuity. I had been rejected and, quite frankly, I thought I deserved the pain I felt after what I had done to my "high-school sweetheart." However, I couldn't exist alone. By now, I thought sex was love and I needed to feel desired. Being drunk dulled the senses and cast away my inhibitions. I made drinks and drugs my bandages against the pain. My "bandages" led me further and further into self-deception. I partied from Thursday to Monday morning, feeling that at least a few days ought to be respectable. I was failing out of school and driving myself into prostitution.

Oh, I believed I was the life of the party. People laughed at my jokes, and I was very popular, invited to parties every weekend. I danced and sang well into the night before I fell into bed with someone, anyone. I stopped counting. Remembering names was impossible. All the boys thought I was desirable. After a night of passion, they would give me gifts. I was very special.

The reality was I was a sloppy drunk; happy, but loud and obnoxious. People did not laugh with me but at me. I was the evening's entertainment. Since I was also very willing, I was passed around from bed to bed as the night's entertainment. I would wake up wondering who the guy was this time. Then they started paying me for sex with gifts. Oh, I was special, alright!

Every morning the latest guy would leave, and there was nothing again, so I started over. This was a vicious circle of undeniable desire for validation and a soul broken for lack of it. My willingness to live in woundedness had spiraled into self-destruction. I didn't see it that way, but that was the reality.

A thief has only one thing in mind – he wants to steal, slaughter, and destroy. (John 10:10a)

Satan is this thief and any self-made defense I hid behind he used against me. In ignorance or foolishness, I continuously bandaged my own wounds hoping for relief, never realizing that my thoughts and actions were the very things hurting me. This was no balm for healing. Since the walls I built around my heart and soul were freely accessible to the enemy, my relief never came. And since God will not force Himself on a person, He waited. . .

I was like that turtle. Imagine having this satisfactory existence, swimming and eating and being amphibious. Then one day while swimming along and minding your own business; a net comes and catches you. Maybe you're scared for a little while, but a kind set of hands "rescues" you and now you're in a new environment that isn't so bad. There's food and water. No swimming, but you're amphibious; you can adjust. You're not free, but life's alright. Settling into your new home, you adjust. You meet the neighbors, lobsters in a tank beside you. No longer are you who you were meant to be, but it's all good.

What you can't see is the kitchen around the corner. The specialty is turtle soup, and you're the next course. Suddenly, those "kind" hands pick you up and move you to a noisy place with very sharp knives. You're on your back flailing your legs around to escape, but you're not going anywhere. The pot's boiling. It's just a matter of time. The life you thought was reality was no-where near the truth. Now reality is laughing in your face, and you are helpless in this kitchen of hell. This terrific life would be mine for the foreseeable future.

But we're never alone. God's sees reality, too. He sees us ravaged by sin and ruining ourselves. But He also sees us as we could be, and He never stops trying to rescue us from our mess.

"Why will you be beaten anymore? Will you continue the revolt? The whole head is sick, and the whole heart is faint. From the sole of the foot to the head, no soundness is in it; only a wound and a stripe and a fresh blow, they have not been closed, nor bound up, nor was it softened with oil. . . Come now and let us reason together, says Jehovah; though your sins are as scarlet, they shall be white as snow; though they are red as the crimson, they shall be like wool. If you are willing and hear, you shall eat the good of the land. But if you refuse and rebel, you shall be devoured with the sword; for the mouth of Jehovah has spoken." (Isaiah 1:7, 15-17)

These words could have been a balm for me; the reasonable, quiet love of God showing me what life could be.

But I have come to give you everything in abundance, more than you expect – life in its fullness until you overflow! (John 10:10b)

This is not an angry God judging us harshly because of our sins. He walks into our hell's kitchen and sees clearly and completely our situation. He turns to us and says, "Why are you putting yourself through this? Can't you see how completely dangerous this is?! Talk to Me. See how I can heal you? If you come with Me, I will bless you and save you from this death. If you stay, they're going to eat you eventually."

We can see this analogy because we understand cooking. Things must die to make our food. Our perspective is complete because we are the cook. The carrot does not know it will be chopped and eaten, but we know its fate because we are more than a carrot and in control of the cooking pot.

But what if we're the carrot ...

Is not God more than us? His perspective is complete because He *is* the Creator. He can see a bigger picture we cannot even conceive. So, when He enlightens us to our fate if we persist in our lifestyle of sin, we may hear it as judgmental, but He is merely telling us the consequences of our actions.

I needed to hear His voice. I desperately needed to be guided by Him. Although I didn't say this prayer out loud, God heard my heart and walked right into the hell I was in and waited ...

Natural Consequences can have a high price.

I had walked into my life as a drunken whore because my heart was broken too many times. I needed to feel loved so badly it consumed me. But my need led me to quick solutions that had no depth. When this boy, who had sworn he would marry me after he finished sowing his wild oats, started to date my roommate I came unglued, but what was I supposed to do with all this emotion? I had agreed to this insanity, so I kept it in believing his lies of, "Let's see other people before we marry." The one hope that sustained me through all the debauchery was that in the end, I would be special to him forever. (I read this now and can't believe I believed that!)

One afternoon I came home to discover their lovemaking. They had promised not to have sex in our apartment, and here they were throwing it in my face. I quietly walked to my room, shut the door, and sat on the bed wishing the walls were thicker. I listened to him say to her the very words he had said to me. The same wooing and promises he was making to her; he had made to me. The same passionate embraces were now hers to enjoy. When they finished, they moved through the house like nothing was wrong. They laughed and talked as they fixed themselves something to eat and settled into the living room to enjoy some TV. I lost my sanity.

I sat there envisioning myself going into the kitchen for the sharpest knife in the house and moving toward this man to slit his throat. In this daydream, I watched with joy as his lifeblood drained out onto the floor, his lover screaming in the background. Every detail was intense. Every dying breath was a moment of satisfaction.

In reality, I took a deep breath, and, shaking down to my boots, moved out into the living room. Every ounce of strength was devoted to self-control. Trembling, I managed to speak, telling them to leave or I didn't know what would happen. Apparently, I made quite an impression because they immediately left.

When I returned to my room, the reality of how close I came to murder was too much. It was horrifying to feel happiness when I imagined him dying. The intensity of this fantasy meant I could no longer to be trusted. All my life, I had fought to keep sanity, but now it was truly and finally gone.

"And Jehovah says, "Because the daughters of Zion are proud and walk with stretched out necks and wanton eyes, walking and mincing as they go, and make a tinkling with their feet; therefore, Jehovah will make the crown of the daughter of Zion scabby, and Jehovah will lay all their secret parts bare... And it shall be instead of a smell of perfume, there shall be an odor of decay. And instead of a sash, a rope. And instead of well-set hair, baldness. . .a scar instead of beauty" (Isaiah 3:16-25)

When God speaks the truth is revealed. Hidden things are un-covered. All the finery that we hide behind is now exposed for the lies they are. This was it, my life uncovered! Scabs, decay, scars, baldness – this was a picture of me. I saw my sin, my shame clearly. There is no dressing up depravity. It is repulsive in every way.

I decided I must kill myself. There were no redeeming qualities left. I was just a danger to society. The best thing to do was to rid the world of this menace once and for all.

Suddenly, I was filled with peace. It was such a wonderful feeling to be free of cloying needs and screaming wounds. I was utterly taken in by this false sense of "rightness," and it drove me into certainty about my decision.

Without God, everything we build falls in ruins around us. But when we come to the end of ourselves, God says,

"Come now and let us reason together. Though your sins are like scarlet, they shall be as white as snow. Though they are red like crimson, they shall be as wool. If you are willing and obedient, you shall eat the good of the land. But if you refuse and rebel, you shall be devoured by the sword." (Isaiah 1:18-19)

God was speaking, but I couldn't hear past my faults. Redemption was not in the picture. And so, He was still waiting in this hellish kitchen with me. He saw the danger I was in. This quietness was the lull before the storm, the pause of a raised hammer poised to crack my shell and toss me into the boiling water. I was not in a peaceful place at all!

But in this quietness, He began to speak, to "reason" with me. Every vehicle I chose to die with, He convinced me it was not going to work.

- I could jump off a building. "The tallest building is only three stories. You'll just hurt yourself."
- I could starve myself. "There's food all around. That will take too long, and you'll eventually start eating again."
- I could shoot myself. "You have no money. You don't know anyone with a gun. How are you going to do that?"
- I could walk in front of a moving vehicle. "This is a sleepy college town. No vehicles are moving fast enough to kill you."
- I could sleep around for drugs and then overdose. "You've worn out that road. Why will they give you drugs when you'll do it for free?"
- I will slit my wrists... .

That one He didn't answer. I sat in confusion. For weeks I had been planning and debating always meeting resistance. Now – silence. So, I figured "success!"

I started to get up to get a razor, and I heard, "No."

It was so intense I was convicted. The weight of that "No" kept me sitting right where I was and started a conversation that saved my life.

"Why not?"

"It will crush your parents. They will not understand and forever blame themselves."

I pondered that reply, knowing the absolute truth of it and feeling the regret of hurting them so badly. At that moment it was enough.

"OK. I'll stop for now, but if You want me to live, You'll have to give me more reasons than that."

God met me where I was and began to pull me away from the hell I had embraced. He walked right into my darkest thoughts to spend weeks debating the pros and cons of suicide with me so He could bring me to the point where I could hear a reason to live and accept it. This was the beginning of my "unlearning."

There is no place He won't go for us. He is standing in front of us unaffected by the evil all around, focusing His love on us. Isaiah tells us repeatedly, "His hand is stretched out still" offering deliverance, revelations of love, and freedom from oppression.

Our God is a loving God longing to be intimate with His children. If we fall and turn to Him, He will pick us up and restore us. If we sin and repent, He will forgive and cleanse us. He does this because He knows our weakness and wants to become our strength. He does this because He knows our frailty and wants to give us His joy and peace. He does this because He is love and will not relent until His love causes us to love Him, too.

"We are more than conquerors through Him who loved us. For I am persuaded that neither death nor life, nor angels nor principalities nor powers, nor things present nor things to come, nor height nor depth, nor any other created thing, shall be able to separate us from the love of God which is in Christ Jesus our Lord."
(Romans 8:38-39)

DIGGING DEEPER

- **Read John 10:10**. Recall a situation when Satan tried to destroy your life or attacked you in some way. How did Jesus save/help you?

- **Read Isaiah 1: 18-19**. What is God's response to our sin? How has Jesus made our sins "white as snow?"

- **Read Romans 8: 58-59.** List all of the things that can come between you and God. Praise Him for His faithfulness.

Knowing God through the rules

"I've got my eye on the goal, where God is beckoning us onward – to Jesus. I'm off and running, and I'm not turning back. So let's keep focused on that goal, those of us who want everything God has for us. If any of you have something else in mind, something less than total commitment, God will clear your blurred vision – you'll see it yet! Now that we're on the right track let's stay on it." (Philippians 3: 14-16, MSG)

This is where God began to guide me. Oh, I had learned about rules. They were for show, a list of things that got approval from others. The ones that gained me smiles were good. The ones that didn't were bad.

But God began to love me in ways I didn't understand. Suddenly, I wanted to follow only those rules that made <u>Him</u> smile. When I did, I was content. No more desperate acts to draw attention to myself. No more insecurity measuring people's reactions toward me.

"Come, and let us go up to the mount of Jehovah, to the house of the God of Jacob. And He will teach from His ways, and we will walk in His paths. For out of Zion the law will go forth, and the word of Jehovah from Jerusalem." (Isaiah 2:3)

Laws had always been punitive and strict, and I had always judged myself poorly. But now my eyes were being opened to a different way.

Maybe rules could be part of healing and redemption?

When we begin our walk it's all about rules. Do this, don't do that. It's small, but it is something we can understand. The difference between right and wrong is a beginning concept we can wrap our brains around. From here, we can grow. This was the beginning of my journey to God's heart.

> For precept must be upon precept, precept upon precept, line upon line, line upon line. Here a little, there a little. (Isaiah 28:10)

Isaiah had to learn this in the beginning of his ministry. He knew the rules of living as a son of God. He could see the sin of Israel and Judah because he knew right from wrong. There was white and there was black. His words for them were full of judgment:

> "Woe sinful nation, a people heavy with iniquity; a seed of evildoers, sons who corrupt! They have forsaken Jehovah, they have scorned the Holy One of Israel." (Isaiah 1:4)

> "For Jerusalem has stumbled, and Judah has fallen; because their tongue and their deeds toward Jehovah are to rebel against the eyes of His glory. The look of their faces answers against them; they have declared their sin like Sodom, they do not hide it. Woe to their soul! For they have dealt evil to themselves." (Isaiah 3:8-9)

"Woe" to those who sin and that seems to be everybody! Oh, I could relate. I never had good words to say for myself. Always seeing my "dark side," I entertained thoughts of "Woe to you" every day.

Rules are designed to show right from wrong. It is our choice how we deal with that knowledge. Isaiah judged the people harshly, I judged myself harshly, but God always answered with words of deliverance.

> "Zion shall be redeemed with justice, and her returning ones with righteousness." (Isaiah 1:27)

> "In that day the branch of Jehovah will be beautiful and glorious, and the fruit of the earth for pride and for glory for the survivors of Israel. And it shall be, he remaining in Zion, and he who is left in Jerusalem, shall be called holy." (Isaiah 4:2-3a)

God's message is repentance and deliverance. The message of a loving God who wants to save His people from themselves. He does not deny that our sin is great, but it is always, "Face your sin and repent, and walk into My glory." This is a message of the heart, but Isaiah understood God only through the rules. Although the rules opened his eyes to the right and wrong of life and made God his moral compass, it wasn't enough for him to influence the people or pray effectively for his nation. He began to hear the Lord, but it was only the start of his journey. Now his "unlearning" would begin.

Like Isaiah, it was time for me to "go up to the mount of Jehovah" and unlearn some things. God had come to my world to get me, I needed to explore His to meet Him. He began to show me the value of living by His rules, embracing the narrow road of right. I wasn't ready to feel any deep emotion, so He led me to a deeper connection with music – using it as a balm. Miraculously, I hadn't flunked out of college yet, and now I would practice long into the night, singing myself into healing. I threw myself into study. All those classes I had blown off to party or play needed to be repeated. I had some dues to pay.

Starting from the beginning, I drank the milk of scripture, going back to the basics: God loves me. Jesus gave Himself for me. The ten commandments are good guidelines for living. God is faithful. Building my faith back "line upon line, precept upon precept." (Isaiah 28:10)

He called me to Himself and only Himself. Knowing I would quickly move back into old patterns of need from others, He began to show me just how dangerous that was and how low I had fallen. It was not pretty, and I resolved never to return. I clung to Him. He was my only hope of freedom.

> "If anyone come to Me and does not hate his father and mother, wife and children, brothers and sisters, yes, and his own life also, he cannot be My disciple."
> (Luke 14:26)

We gloss over these verses. "Oh, He didn't mean *hate*. He just meant to put Jesus first." "Jesus was about love, not hate."

Jesus/God/Holy Spirit is not about love. He *is* love. And as we grow in Him, as He changes us to be like Himself, we see the things of this world differently – even the people around us. We might never hate our family, but we will come to a place where their influence over us is gone. We will see that Jesus is more valuable than they are. We will want Jesus more than anything or anyone else. And if someone stands in the way of our relationship with God, then, yes, we will "hate" them; cut ourselves off from them. We will move them aside, even out of our lives, to be with Jesus. When we let go of everything we know and know only Him, He can do a glorious and complete work in us, bringing us to Himself, perfect joy, peace, and love. This is a journey I was just beginning, but there was no doubt that I would travel it.

Following God's rules meant leaving my old lifestyle completely, and that put me in isolation. No longer willing to party, my "friends" considered me an outcast. Everyone else had written me off; no one trusted or paid me any attention. I couldn't blame them; they had good reason. One teacher saw the change and encouraged me; the others couldn't wait until I dropped out. Doors opened to me when I entered college were now closed, and I faced a very narrow journey down a very dark hall.

God became my sanctuary and my guide. I began to study the Bible, and my eyes were opened to the traps and snares I had fallen into. I knew without Him I would fall back again, the temptation to find company at a party was very strong. But the choice to live made me determined to find out why that was a good decision. I dedicated everything I could think of to Him, my life, my music, my possessions, my mind. For months I lived in isolation, walking in a world that didn't see me. For almost two years, I had been a drunk. People still saw me that way.

It takes a while for filth to be washed away. You must soak awhile and learn to live cleanly. Habits must change. Language must change. But God is relentless in His works and bit by bit He was cleansing me from the caked-on dirt of my life so far.

> "In that day the branch of Jehovah will be beautiful and glorious, and the fruit of the earth for pride and for glory for the survivors of Israel. And it shall be, he remaining in Zion, and he who is left in Jerusalem, shall be called holy, everyone who is written among the living in Jerusalem; when the Lord shall have washed away the filth of the daughters of Zion. . . Then Jehovah will create a cloud and smoke by day, and the shining of a flaming fire by night, for over all the site of Mount Zion, and over her assemblies; for over all the glory will be a canopy. And they shall be a booth for a shade by day from the heat, and for a refuge, and for a hiding-place from storm and rain." (Isaiah 4:2-6)

Our God is a loving God, longing to be intimate with His People. If we fall and turn to Him, He will pick us up and restore us. If we sin and repent, He will forgive and cleanse us. He does this because He knows our weakness and wants to become our strength. He does this because He knows our frailty and wants to give us His joy and peace. He does this because He is love and will not relent until this love He gives us causes us to love Him, too.

> "We love Him because He first loved us."
> (1 John 4:19)

His "cloud by day" and "fire by night" is a direct reference to how His presence was manifested for Israel in the days of Moses when they were wandering in the wilderness. God led them and dwelt with them, providing their every need and victory in conflict. He was ever-present for His people, wanting to share a relationship with them.

Jesus was doing for me what He had been doing for His people since time began, and what He will keep doing forever. He is the beautiful and glorious branch of Jehovah who will "wash away the filth of the daughters of Zion." He had washed off the filth of drunkenness and promiscuity from me, and now I was moving under His cloud and fire. I lived a solitary life alone, but it was just a matter of time before His presence around me began to draw some attention.

DIGGING DEEPER

- Name a few Biblical rules that have helped you in life. What do they show you about God's nature?

- Have you ever reached a point of "unlearning?" What happened?

- **Read Luke 14:26.** What do you think Jesus means when He says, "You must hate your mother and father?"

- **Read Isaiah 4: 2-6.** What words or phrases stood out to you in this scripture? What do you think God is saying to you through them?

Understanding through experience

"Then I looked, and I heard the voice of many angels around the throne, the living creatures, and the elders; and the number of them was ten thousand times ten thousand, and thousands of thousands, saying with a loud voice: "Worthy is the Lamb who was slain to receive power and riches and wisdom and strength and honor and glory and blessing!" And every creature which is in heaven and on the earth and under the earth and such as are in the sea, and all that are in them, I hear saying: "Blessing and honor and glory and power be to Him who sits on the throne, and to the Lamb, forever and ever!"
(Revelation 5:11-13)

Until now, Isaiah and I knew the rules and saw the sin but didn't really know God. This was about to change for both of us.

In the 6th chapter of Isaiah, he sees God in person on His throne surrounded by amazing angels. All Isaiah can hear is the angels shouting praise so loudly that the whole place is shaking, and he is overcome by his unworthiness!

"In the year that King Uzziah died, then I saw the Lord sitting on a throne, high and lifted up. And the train filled the temple. Above it stood the seraphs. Each one had six wings, with two he covered his face; and with two he covered his feet; and with two he flew. And one cried to the other and said, 'Holy, holy, holy is Jehovah of hosts; all the earth is full of His glory!' And the doorposts shook from the voice of the one who cried, and the house was filled with smoke. Then I said, 'Woe is me! For I am cut off; for I am a man of unclean lips, and I live amongst a people of unclean lips; for my eyes have seen the King, Jehovah of hosts." (Isaiah 6:1-5)

In the presence of God, we see the reality of who we are. Isaiah was a righteous man but standing before God he realized he had no right to be there. The pure holiness of God shone right through him and revealed his sin like the sun reveals the earth. Through that revelation came the realization that all the sacrifices of Israel would not be enough to save him, much less the nation. Unless God intervened, all was lost. He knew only the rules. He had no experience of God's mercy.

"Then one of the seraphs flew to me with a live coal in his hand, snatched with tongs from the altar. And he touched it on my mouth, and said, 'See, this has touched your lips and your iniquity is taken away, and your sin is covered." (Isaiah 6: 6-7)

God's mercy touches Isaiah through the fire and the sacrifices on the altar. Nothing he did or could have done would have sanctified him. Freely, God purified him to relieve his distress and cause him to connect with God in a new, more intimate way. It is an undeserved offering of God's mercy.

Here is Jesus on the cross for us. His sacrifice, His life laid down on the altar of God, is what we receive. The intensity of His holiness is what touches us and burns away our sin. I had been redeemed, but I had no idea of the magnitude of this gift of God. Isaiah did nothing to merit sanctification, I had certainly done nothing to deserve it, God just gave it. We can do nothing to deserve Jesus. Out of His love God just gives Him to us.

"And I heard the voice of Jehovah saying, 'Whom shall I send, and who will go for Us?' Then I said, 'I am here. Send me!'" (Isaiah 6:8)

And now Isaiah can hear God. Transformed by His glory and moved by His request, Isaiah forgets his fear and immediately approaches God to volunteer himself. A minute ago, he was so afraid; he thought he was going to die! The transforming power of God is miraculous. His love conquers our fears, and we desire to please Him. If we accept the heat of His refining and the touch of His cleansing sanctification, we can be changed into glory.

Salvation is always here. Isaiah will witness the devastation, genocide, and enslavement of his people; but his hope will be in "the holy seed" left in the remnant of the Israelites.

The entirety of my life so far was destroyed, and my mind crushed. Now my hope was in "the holy seed" growing slowly in my heart. Even though Isaiah and I didn't know this Jesus, our hearts moved past the rules and our hope was now in Christ all the same.

We can follow all the rules, but they are just the beginning. An encounter with God touches us in ways we cannot easily explain and changes us forever. Rules can't do that. They do show us aspects of God, and that is good, but rules are not the personal relationship God is wanting; they are the preparation for a deeper love, and God was moving me in.

Moving into fellowship

There were some Christian women who had been my friends when I was able to hide my debauchery, but when my sin became plain, they had walked away from me. I understood. I had thoroughly abandoned everything they held dear and rejected them totally. Now they watched as I stopped skipping class and arrived sober and on time. They saw me practicing those long hours and noticed me begin to talk intelligently during discussions. No longer needing to perform for friends, I submitted to authority and stopped hurling insults under my breath.

One day they approached me, and tentatively asked how I was doing. I was so surprised I stammered and was immediately suspicious of what they were up to. Well, they were up to inviting me to church! As soon as I was alone, I cried tears of gratitude. Was I finally being accepted? Was this the beginning of a family of friends who cared about me? God had moved them to approach me, and I clung to this refuge with all my might.

Their church was raucous, filled with the young energy of college students, and I loved it! They met in an old barn at the end of a dirt road. A farmer had donated it to this fledgling congregation, and I dove in: worship, Bible studies, Christian study groups, pizza after rehearsals. I could laugh without alcohol and love friends without sex.

I would never have found that church tucked away in the middle of nowhere. God brought me there, knowing it was just what I needed. It was my home until I finally graduated. I learned how to act like a Christian. I learned the value of following after righteousness with my mind and body. I knew the dangers of sin; now I learned how to live without them. I began to find fulfillment in the goodness of God.

Just when I thought it was going well. . .

> "Although we live in the natural realm, we don't wage a military campaign employing human weapons, using manipulation to achieve our aims. Instead, our spiritual weapons are energized with divine power to effectively dismantle the defenses behind which people hide. We can demolish every deceptive fantasy that opposes God and break through every arrogant attitude that is raised up in defiance of the true knowledge of God. We capture, like prisoners of war, every thought and insist that it bow in obedience to the Anointed One."
> (2 Corinthians 10:3-4, TPT)

I was all in; had made a life commitment and retreat was not an option. I had given Jesus all my things, truly dedicated to the Lord for His will. I loved Him and vowed to live a life of virtue. I was on my way to being a good Christian. My life would be a testimony of victory!

I felt healed, but God knew the truth. My pride told me I was saved; now all was good, and I could continue on my own. But even though my soul was God's, I still held on to my past, unwilling to let go of all the insights I had gained over the years. After all, our experiences bring us wisdom, right? My wounds still oozed insecurity and foolishness.

Fresh out of college, I was offered a position in China at a missionary school teaching English to children. I also was seriously considering a call into the ministry. What did I do? I married an abusive man. My need to be punished (a need that had been instilled in me all my life) was front and center, and I was led by it. Of course, I was a master of blame-shifting. "Those people don't understand." "I'm being persecuted because I stand for love." "He'll change with the love of a good woman. I just have to persevere, and happiness will come." "He didn't mean it. He's just a damaged soul who needs love. I'm doing a good work."

I remember the morning after we were married. I woke up to a soft morning light through the window and snuggled up to him, happy to have the very first morning of our lives together. He pushed me away and said, "Come on, Joy. We're married. We don't have to pretend anymore." That was the high point of our relationship. Public humiliation, violent outbursts of temper, demanding expectations, low opinions of me, it took a lot of self-deception to convince myself that this was going to work out.

I stayed with him for 4 years until my son was born. After all, in the eyes of the world, we were successful. He and I were both teachers; we lived in a nice home, had two cars, wanted for nothing. I could hide behind the façade of happiness and success. The world didn't need to know the truth. But when my son was born, I found myself blaming my beautiful baby for my sadness. I believed an innocent baby, wholly dependent on my care, was manipulating the world against me. Oh my. . . . I looked in the mirror and saw a woman in great need of some professional help.

The enemy had made some pretty big strongholds in my mind, and they didn't come out without a fight. *Don't let them really know you. They won't like what they see. It's self-preservation to keep my emotional distance.* (that was about 50 miles!) *No one knows what's best for me but me. Don't trust anyone.*

I began to realize that the defenses I had created to protect myself, that I thought were a good thing, were twisting my opinions and negatively influencing my judgment. My beautiful son showed me just how much ugliness I still had to deal with. At the time, I was still living in my hometown, and my mother was working at a Christian counseling center. I asked her if I could become a client, and she introduced me to Martha, the woman who led me into mental health.

Our meetings began civilly. I would come prepared with "the problem of the week." She and I would talk about it, and I would leave feeling better. But, eventually, I realized that this was just me trying to control our sessions, and I wasn't going to get better if it continued. (*Hmmm. Do you think that was God?*) One day I arrived, sat down, and said nothing. She encouraged me to begin, and I told her that I was no longer going to do that. I needed her to tell me what to do. She was the professional, and I was now willing to be guided by her expertise. She smiled. Now the work could begin.

During that time of counseling, I grew in courage and resolve while I faced some deep fears and began to allow God to heal gaping wounds of grief and pain. It was here in my life that my father and I began to heal. He had been an absent father, constantly at church for rehearsals, meetings, or working in his office. He loved us, but time with him was fleeting and rare. Soon after my son and I started life on our own, dad approached me in private and asked for forgiveness for neglecting me. He was sincerely sorry that he couldn't go back in time and make it right, but, if I was willing, he wanted to be a good grandfather to my son. I burst into tears of joy, and we hugged each other for a while. There was no way I would deny him that, and watching him create and maintain a loving, nurturing relationship with my son, and I was one of the most healing experiences of my life.

I have always processed things in daydreams and visions, part of being a seer. This counseling experience was no exception. I remember while Martha and I were working through a deep hurt, I kept envisioning myself kneeling on a frozen lake. There was a big black "blob" pulsating just under the ice. I was watching it while holding an ice pick, stabbing and picking at the ice right above it. I saw the thing clearly and was afraid of it but was more determined to break the ice between us.

After weeks of pick, pick, picking, I was driving home from my latest session and the ice cracked through, and that thing exploded out; a tidal wave of darkness passing right through me. I parked the car and let it happen. It seemed never to end, and I was overcome with fear, grief, shame, so many negative emotions all I could do was collapse and sob and scream. I didn't know what was happening, except that blackness was all around like a freight train running me over. Then - it was gone, and a feeling of peace came over me, the depth of which I had never known. There was joy, too; not a bubbly happiness, but a current of strength and contentment I had never experienced before. I was exhausted, but I was free.

"When the enemy comes in like a flood, the Spirit of the Lord will lift up a standard against him."
(Isaiah 59: 19)

Well, the enemy had certainly done that! And the Lord had most certainly lifted up protection around me, giving Martha wisdom as she helped me live in this new way of being. Now I had a new mind; full of compassion, but strong enough to face worldly realities. I found the demanding need for people's affection and approval was quieted, and I had even more peace. My son's need for me was no longer a burden but a blessing. His vulnerability was an opportunity to love rather than a cause to fear. I began to learn how to rest in this new peace.

The future I had built in my marriage for myself and my son

was not healthy and needed to change. I convinced my husband to go with me for marriage counseling, but it failed miserably, and I was not willing to submit to abuse anymore. This new compassion born out of my deliverance let me love my husband more than I ever had, but also gave me hope for a healthy life for my son and me. I left, and the relationship fell apart.

The next few years were full of ups and downs. The separation from my child's father was contentious. The changes I was going through in therapy made sustaining my job impossible, and they let me go. But the little house God found for me was delightful, right by the water in a quiet neighborhood. My new church was very much like the barn, full of life and joy.

My prayer life was the most special. In the evening, after my son was asleep, I would read my Bible and ponder scripture. I began to read William Barclay's commentaries on the New Testament as daily devotionals and found Jesus in deeper revelations of familiar scripture.

I really didn't know how to pray, so I would pray in tongues. Jesus would meet me there in experiences of enveloping love. My struggling heart would feel His comfort and strength. My confusion and guilt would be quieted in His peace. Time alone was time spent knowing Him, and His light kept me centered and sane.

"The people who walk in darkness have seen a great light. The ones who dwell in the land of the shadow of death – Light has shone on them." (Isaiah 9:2)

No matter how dark and threatening our lives get, there is the Light that cannot be put out; that shines in the deepest darkness. Jesus is the Light that breaks off depression, frees us from oppression, heals all our wounds and disease – the miracle-working power of God's Light.

These experiences of intimacy were opening me up. As He opened me to Himself, He also opened me to myself. My counselor, Martha, continued to press into my wounds. I had been formally diagnosed as clinically depressed and within that diagnosis was an unhealthy chasm between my thoughts and my emotions.

My psyche had been shattered, and I felt as though "all the king's horses and all the king's men couldn't put [Joy] together again." But my King was going to do it!

God began to bridge this chasm in dreams and visions. I remember during one session, I had a vision of a small girl, about 5 or 6, huddled in the corner of a dark room. It was like a ramshackle shack falling down around her with big gaps in the walls. There were no windows, just the shadowy light that slipped through cracks. Her clothes were so old they were in tatters. She hadn't bathed in a very long time. She huddled there in silence. She had passed the point of hoping for rescue or care. She was limp with despair and didn't see me looking at her. For many months I just stood at a distance and looked. At one point she looked up at me, and the faint, painful hope in her eyes was too much to bear, but still, I didn't move.

I didn't realize it, but Martha knew this was "the child inside me," and I needed to connect again with those emotions I had walled up to protect myself. This vision, this little girl was God's way of showing me a part of myself. All those "words of wisdom" I had adopted were actually curses that hurt me deep inside. "Don't get too close to anyone" was really "Everyone will hurt you. You better be afraid and hide." "I am the smartest person in the room" was really "Separate yourself from everyone because no one is really your friend." Fears constantly tortured me until the only way to exist was to put all my emotions away and live in my intellect. This abused little girl was those isolated emotions personified, and I had not been facing them in any way.

But Martha was relentless, poking, and prodding me into healing. Every time she led me back to hurt or trauma, I felt the sting of fear and sadness as though it was the first time. I forced myself to handle it all and took everything to Jesus in prayer. I couldn't heal myself. I mean, I had created this mess! At least I knew that much. But He was faithful to soothe my wounds and closer and closer we all moved toward freedom and connection for that poor little girl and me.

Finally came the day of the breakthrough. I don't remember precisely the last wound, but I do remember my heart finally breaking for this abused child. I could hold back no more. I approached her and sat down, asking for permission just to hold her. She crawled into my lap and curled into my arms. We just sat there together. No tears, just quietness, and connection. I was coming back to myself, merging the pieces of brokenness back together. Every year brought more and more healing; even through mistakes and backsliding, I learned to love this child, moving slowly but surely into wholeness.

These experiences were so powerful. I thought they were "it," but God had much more in mind for me. Experience is only another step towards completeness.

If I had answered His continuing call to "Come now and let us reason together" things would have gone better. But I was lost in experiencing this new life. I was discovering depths of healing and love I had never known. Wanting to stay in these experiences forever, I ignored God's call to even deeper intimacy. I convinced myself I was at the pinnacle of joy. My heart was open, and I loved the whole world! But this happiness was temporary. My ability to care for myself was not complete. My self-indulgence would be my downfall.

DIGGING DEEPER

- **Read Isaiah 9:2.** Can you think of a time when God's light shone for you? Have you ever experienced a day of breakthrough? What happened?

- **Read Isaiah 58:19.** What does this scripture tell you about God's love for you?

- **Remember a time when you "experienced" God.** What happened? What did you learn about God in those moments?

Understanding through love

"Beloved, while I was very diligent to write to you concerning our common salvation, I found it necessary to write to you exhorting you to contend earnestly for the faith which was once for all delivered to the saints."
(Jude 3)

I had been healed of many things, but it was not done. I had found peace in inner healing and my pride and defenses worked very hard to convince me that this newfound joy was the end. I saw the world differently, with more compassion and reveled in the newfound peace and strength that was mine. I held on to that belief because I was weary of the process and wanted to stop.

It was just a different perspective in self-centered thinking. When we get lost in our own thoughts and understanding of God and the world, we are headed for trouble. Our self-absorption leads us to pride, and our hearts are deceived. But if our lives are built on faith, God will save us from ourselves. This is a lesson I was about to learn.

I was not a good mother. I just didn't know how to be nurturing. I loved my son but fumbled around trying to express it in healthy ways. I stumbled, groped, and never really got the hang of it. Feeling out of my depth, I resolved to find another husband who could fix the situation. This seemed wise to me. Why not share this newfound joy with someone else? My self-loathing seemed to be gone, but my twisted thoughts about love were still there. Feeling healed, I determined my need for Jesus wasn't so great, and I could begin to make decisions on my own. My pride was in evidence even then.

I did make one wise decision and shielded my son from the men I was dating. But I was still driven by the fear that if I didn't "perform," the relationship would end. I was monogamous (an improvement from the past), but I was an insecure single mother looking for prince charming to rescue me. Society provided my excuse. In the eighties, being with only one man was considered high morals, and these feelings were "normal" to me. I didn't realize there was something wrong with this thought process.

My desperation eventually drove me right into the arms of a married man. Well, that didn't go well. He confessed his marriage after he knew I was completely in love. I twisted and turned in the winds of his deception, needing to feel that what I was doing was OK. I believed the lies he told me: "My marriage is a sham and means nothing." "We sleep in separate rooms. It's not really a marriage." "If I had met you before I would never have married her, but now I'm trapped."

I chose to walk down that road of death, willing to accept an illusion rather than face life on my own. It didn't occur to me to trust Jesus to provide, and all His calls went unanswered as I chased this nightmare fantasy.

Humanity throughout history seems to fall into this pit. Isaiah saw it clearly and sang the song I should have listened to:

> "Now I will sing to my Beloved a song of my Beloved concerning His vineyard: My Beloved has a vineyard in a fruitful horn. And He dug it, and cleared it of stones, and planted it with the choicest vine, and built a tower in its midst, and hewed out a wine vat in it. And He waited for it to produce grapes, but it produced rotten grapes. And now, O people of Jerusalem and men of Judah, I ask you, judge between Me and My vineyard. What more could have been done to My vineyard that I have not done in it? Who knows? I waited for it to yield grapes, but it yielded rotten grapes. And now I will make known

to you what I will do then to My vineyard. I will take away its hedge, and it will be burned, I will breach its wall, and it will become a trampling ground. And I will lay it waste; it shall not be pruned nor hoed; but briars and thorns shall come up. And I will command the clouds from raining rain on it. For the vineyard of Jehovah of hosts is the house of Israel, and the man of Judah is His delightful plant. And He waited for justice, but behold, bloodshed; for righteousness, but behold, a cry! (Isaiah 5:1-7)

This was my story. God did everything right. He picked the perfect place and prepared the soil just right. He planted the best of the best vines. He built a tower strong and sure where others would have built a hovel. He even built the wine vat right in the vineyard so the workers could harvest and make wine easily.

Everything was now done. My soul was saved. His temple in me was built. The angels were ready to reap the harvest. All God had to do was wait for His work in me to mature, for the grapes to grow in this perfect environment and reap the harvest. So, He waited, and when it was time for the harvest, there wasn't a decent grape to be had. The whole crop was bad.

Then God asks, "What do you recommend I do now?"

Obviously, the venture failed miserably. It wasn't God's fault. He is the only being who can grow grapes with a free will to be rotten or good. Those grapes had everything they needed to be wonderful, and they *chose* to be rotten! Anybody in their right mind would walk away and start again somewhere else. Anybody else would abandon me to my "sinful ways." I had certainly proven myself unreliable. Once again, I had returned to a life I kept giving up for love of Him.

Experience had only brought me so far. God had created a vineyard for me to grow in, but I abandoned it. The need for validation was still strong and I had processed these experiences right into it. God was loving me in deeper and deeper ways which, in my mind, made me special, set apart, able to understand life in amazing ways others just couldn't. Yes, I had more compassion, and

I was a much better person, but there were still little pains I lived with. What I didn't realize was those little pains were just the bruises from the unconscious needs that were still bleeding. God was after complete healing, and I had stopped at the door.

I was that vineyard personified. God had given me a new mind and heart and I had neglected them for an old lifestyle and belief system. I had followed the rules, grown into new experiences, but my needs and fears were stronger than my will to do right. My experience of His love was twisted by my ideas of "normal" and "acceptable," and now I was right back where He found me, in that horrible kitchen ready to become turtle soup.

My "boyfriend" was talking about sending my 4-year-old son to boarding school so we could travel together. I was so deep into it by this time that I seriously considered it! I was tearing apart, trying to love God, my son, and this man at the same time. I had turned away from God's covenant of life and accepted a death sentence from Satan. This man demanded my total devotion. He resented my time with my son and Jesus. Pulling me further and further into his web, he reduced me to complete weakness and isolation. On the verge of a nervous breakdown, I watched my life crumble away - again.

"So hear the word of Jehovah, scornful man, rulers of the people in Jerusalem. Because you have said, 'We have cut a covenant with death' and 'We have made a vision with Sheol – when the overwhelming rod passes through, it will not come to us, for we have made the lie our refuge, and we have hidden in falsehood.'" (Isaiah 28:15)

At the root was pride. I really believed I could handle life on my own, from my own wisdom. That was my "covenant with death." I was going to church but depending on myself. I was praying and hearing God's guidance, but not really listening. I was reading the Bible, but only for the sake of self-validation. Now my life was out of control, I saw no way out and collapsed in defeat. I thought I had won, but I had done it again, failed utterly.

But God. . .

> "Behold, I lay in Zion a stone for a foundation. A tried stone, a precious cornerstone, a sure foundation; whoever believes will not act hastily. Also I will make justice the measuring line, and righteousness the plummet; the hail will sweep away the refuge of lies, and the waters will overflow the hiding place. Your covenant with death will be annulled. And your agreement with Sheol will not stand." (Isaiah 28:16-18)

It was the nature of Israel to turn away from God constantly. I always wondered why they would do that, never learning their lesson, and yet, here I was doing the same thing time and again. Now God had to take matters into His own hands. Because I refused to hear the Lord; because I believed I knew what I was doing and didn't need a relationship with Him, He – Himself – built the foundation I so vehemently resisted.

His precious Cornerstone will always be faithful because it is Himself sacrificed for us. Everything built on it will be measured and plumbed by justice and righteousness. That hailstorm that looked so frightening will be a cleansing force, sweeping away sin and deception. The power of death will be broken, and the curse that should be our future will never be.

That is God's promise. At the depth of my despair, I turned to God, laying my life before Him and admitting I was a screw-up. I freely confessed I was in over my head and needed Him to intervene. I met with my pastor and told him all. He was shocked but gave me the best advice – "Get out. Get out now! Tell no one you're leaving. Call someone you absolutely trust and just pack up and go." I called my dad, and he dropped everything and flew across the country to save me.

"And it shall be in that day, Jehovah shall thresh from the channel of the River to the torrent of Egypt; and you shall be gathered one by one, sons of Israel. And it shall be in that day, the great trumpet shall be blown; and those perishing in the land of Assyria and the outcasts in the land of Egypt shall come, and shall worship Jehovah in the holy mountain in Jerusalem." (Isaiah 27:13)

God is busy bringing all His children home to safety. He searches the world and culls out His children from the places where they are perishing. Bless the goodness of God; I was no exception.

It took my brother and my dad just two days to pack up my whole life. Before I knew it, my dad, my son, my cat and I were in a rental truck and on our way. This was not a grand adventure. I was terrified that I would be found out and forcibly returned. I cried or trembled with panic through the first two days. The only things that kept me from complete collapse were my son, my father's voice, and the need to drive. I hung on to the passing miles and the thought that growing distance would bring me safety.

I think back now and realize that God had never abandoned me. Left to my own devices, I was a wreck. But as soon as I reached out for help, He was there making it possible for me to start life anew once more.

" And it shall be in that day, the Lord shall again set His hand, the second time, to recover the remnant of His people that remains, . . .And He shall lift up a banner for the nations, and shall gather the outcasts of Israel, and gather those dispersed from Judah, from the four wings of the earth." (Isaiah 11:11-12)

My life in Virginia was in shreds. Twice I had driven myself into hell and twice God had saved me. There was nothing left for me there. Five days and 2500 miles later I limped into Arizona on the arm of my father and collapsed.

I had looked for love in all the places I knew. Now God could show me a better way. A year later, when I finally raised my head and looked around, I saw the love of my family providing for my son and me. I saw another family of people at church who truly cared about our future. There was love all around; good, healthy, caring love. This was new, and I struggled to accept it. As time sent Virginia further and further away, God loved me back to Himself and into the community.

DIGGING DEEPER

- **Read Isaiah 5: 1-7.** Does this story resonate with you? How?

- **Read Isaiah 28: 16-18.** What is God using justice to measure when He says, "I will make justice the measuring line?" If water in the Bible refers to Holy Spirit, what does the work of "hail" and "waters" do in your life? How has Jesus annulled your covenant with death?

Blind faith and the
Garden of Gethsemane

"[Jesus] had to be a Man and take hold of our humanity in every way. He made us His brothers and sisters and became our merciful and faithful King-Priest before God; as the One who removed our sins to make us one with Him. He suffered and endured every test and temptation, so that He can help us every time we pass through the ordeals of life." (Hebrews 2:17-18, TPT)

"I have labored in vain; I have spent My strength for nothing, and in vain." (Isaiah 49:4)

I believe that what Jesus did for us on the cross was bigger than we can imagine. This Lord who was saving me, again and again, has a love beyond reason. Sometimes we just have to back-up and stare in wonder.

When I was a child, church was a big part of our family life. My father was the Director of Music, and my mother was a Sunday School teacher and deacon, so our whole family was heavily involved in the life of the church.

It was a big, established Methodist church. Built in the early 1800s, it mimicked the gothic cathedrals in Europe with high ceilings and lots of ornamental wood. The altar was huge, standing about 15 feet tall on the back wall of a substantial front area that housed two choir lofts, an organ, a piano, two raised lecterns where the Bible was read (on the right) and sermons were preached (on the left), and an empty space in the middle big enough for a chamber orchestra.

Above the altar was a huge stained-glass window of that famous picture of Jesus in the garden of Gethsemane kneeling at a rock with His hands folded in prayer and His face looking up at God. Many was the Sunday I was distracted by that window and wondered what exactly Jesus was praying all night long.

I was taught that He was afraid of the torture and death that was coming, and He was praying for God to "take this cup from Me" and release Him from that suffering part of His ministry, when He sweat blood from the stress it was because of this great fear.

But if Jesus was afraid of physical suffering, He wouldn't have walked mile after mile crossing and re-crossing Israel, sleeping on the ground with rocks for pillows, and saying things that got Him man-handled and physically thrown out of town. He wouldn't have worked as a carpenter until He was thirty, hammering His thumb and bearing the bruises and pain that come with that kind of work, day after day for so many years. I'm not saying that being crucified is a walk in the park, but physical pain was not a stranger to Jesus.

Besides, Jesus was God. He came from heaven (John 6:33) and knew that He was not going to die but rise again to heaven. Why would He be *so* scared of death and pain, knowing it was horrific but very temporary?

When I was older, I learned about the cup of God's wrath. He was about to suffer the full anger of God against the sins of the world. No other man could do it, and if *He* didn't, there would be no redemption for Israel. Only Jesus, who was God, would know the depth of that pain.

But what if there was something else, too? What if God opened a window for us to know what was said there through the mouth of a prophet that lived hundreds of years before Christ? The same prophet that proclaimed Jesus' birth, life, and death could be the one God used to tell us what He and Jesus were saying.

If He did, then Isaiah 49 is a conversation between Jesus and

God. The first 5 verses are Jesus' prayer, and 6-26 are God's answer.

"Come hear Me; and you people from afar, prick up your ear. Jehovah called Me from the womb; He mentioned My name from My mother's belly. And He made My mouth like a sharp sword; He hid Me in the shadow of His hand, and made Me a polished arrow; He hid Me in His quiver; and said to Me, 'You are My servant, Israel, You in whom I shall be glorified.' Then I said, 'I have labored in vain; I have spent My strength for nothing, and in vain; yet surely My judgment is with Jehovah, and My work with My God.' And now says Jehovah who formed Me from the womb to be His servant, to bring Jacob back to Him; 'though Israel is not gathered, yet I am honored in the eye of Jehovah, and My God is My strength.'"
(Isaiah 49:1-5)

It is astounding how much of this prayer is present in the New Testament.

- "Jehovah called me from the womb; He mentioned My name from My mother's belly" is proclaimed by Gabriel in his announcement to Mary; "Behold, you will conceive in your womb and bring forth a Son, and shall call His name Jesus. He will be great, and will be called the Son of the Highest; and the Lord God will give him the throne of His father David. And He will reign over the house of Jacob forever, and of His kingdom there will be no end." (Luke 1: 31-33)

- "He made My mouth like a sharp sword" is witnessed by John: "[Jesus] had in His right hand seven stars, out of His mouth was a sharp two-edged sword, and His countenance was like the sun shining in its strength." (Revelation 1:16)

- "You in whom I will be glorified" was testified to by Jesus Himself; "I have glorified You on the earth. I have finished the work which You have given Me to do. And

61

now, O Father, glorify Me together with Yourself; with the glory which I had with You before the world was." (John 17: 4-5)

- "Jehovah who formed Me. . .to bring [Israel] back to Him" was testified to again by Jesus Himself; "I was not sent except to the lost sheep of the house of Israel." (Matthew 15:24) and again in a burst of emotion: "O Jerusalem, Jerusalem, the one who kills the prophets and stones those who are sent to her! How often I wanted to gather your children together, as a hen gathers her chicks under her wings but you were not willing!" (Matthew 23:37)

And yet in verse 4 Jesus says, "I have labored in vain; I have spent My strength for nothing, and in vain." Why would Jesus say that?

Just before Jesus prays in the Garden of Gethsemane, He gathers with His 12 disciples for the last supper. As He looks around, He sees Judas who will betray Him, Peter who will deny Him, James and John who are bargaining for glory and prestige and another group arguing over who is more important. They are lost in their own desires. Three years of intense training and they just don't get it!

When they move to Gethsemane, He asks them to pray with Him and they keep falling asleep. In that moment His ministry looks like a failure. He was sent to gather all the lost sheep of Israel and all He has managed to do is barely hold this small group of guys together who don't yet understand what He's been teaching and who are about to scatter in fear for their lives. Hardly the outcome He was expecting or working for.

"But," you say, "didn't He know He would rise from the dead and become the Savior of the world?" I believe He knew He would rise because He said so (Luke 24:46), but Jesus didn't know everything (Mark 13:32). God kept certain knowledge from Him, so He could fully experience life as one of us; dependent on God and

Holy Spirit for leadership and wisdom. In that way, His eternal ministry is fulfilled.

> "[Jesus] had to enter into every detail of human life. Then, when He came before God as high priest to get rid of the people's sins, He would have already experienced it all Himself – all the pain, all the testing – and would be able to help where help was needed." (Hebrews 2:17-18 MSG)

Remember the story of the Gentile woman who came to Jesus for a miracle of healing for her daughter? Jesus told her His ministry was not to the Gentiles, but Israel (Matt. 15:21-28). At that time Jesus did not know He would save the whole world, but thought He was here only for the Jews.

Remember the woman with the "issue of blood" who touched the hem of Jesus' robe and was healed? (Mark 5:25-30) Jesus did not know who had touched Him or why. He certainly had not intended to cure anyone at that moment.

Jesus had to face all the temptations we suffer and not sin. "We do not have a High Priest who cannot sympathize with our weaknesses, but was *in all points tempted as we are.*" (Hebrews 4:15, emphasis added) "All" includes seeing reality and not knowing the end. It means He had to live trusting God, not out of His all-knowingness. If we face feeling like a failure and are tempted to throw away the promises of God and go our own way, then He had to as well. All the feelings we struggle with time and time again; frustration, depression, failure, anxiety, anguish. . . He experienced, including total failure!

The "cup" Jesus is holding is the cup of God's wrath. He is facing the moment when He shoulders all the sins of the world and takes the punishment for us. Can we even begin to conceive how excruciating that must have been? No wonder He sweat blood! He's facing the burden of God's complete anger and looking at the fruit of His life in ministry; seeing no successes, nothing to show for it.

All Jesus knew was that He had been sent to bring Israel back to God, and it hadn't happened. Now He's out of time, and He's agonizing about failing not only the people He loves but His Father in heaven who trusted Him with such an important ministry. "I have labored in vain; I have spent My strength for nothing, and in vain." (Isaiah 49:4) He sees nothing but death and continued oppression for His people. "Take this cup from me" (Luke 22:42). What if inside the pain of facing God's wrath is a plea for more time? A breaking heart facing absolute defeat; the collapse of all His hard work?

God brought Him to this point so He could walk through it without sin. This was one of the last temptations Jesus was to face. He had to face the very real possibility that everything He had worked so hard for was nothing; His life a waste of time. All He had was promises that looked empty at this point. The temptation to walk out of that garden and away from the cross must have been overwhelming. He could start over. He could spend more time teaching these disciples. He was still young enough to make something great happen. Maybe, with a stronger ministry behind Him, this cup of wrath would be a little easier to drink? But no, He *did* know that now was the time of His sacrifice.

In the face of His failure, Jesus says, "Yet surely My judgment is with Jehovah and My work with My God. . . I am honored in the eye of Jehovah and My God is My strength." (Isaiah 49:5) Jesus' answer to His own doubts is to stand in faith on His identity in the Father and the promises of God. He does not see or understand how all this is working, but He knows God has a plan and that is enough for Him. "Not My will, but Thine be done." (Luke 22:42)

He has come through this crisis with nothing but trust in His Father. He gives Himself to God's heart, willing to walk to the cross blind to the endgame, every painful step taken in faith.

How does God answer this? It seems He is overcome with love.

"And He said, 'It is too little that You should be My Servant to raise up the tribes of Jacob, and to restore the preserved ones of Israel; I will also give You for a light of the nations, that You may be My salvation to the end of the earth. So says Jehovah, the Redeemer of Israel, His Holy one, to the despised of soul, to the hated of the nation, the servant of rulers. Kings shall see and rise up and chiefs shall worship; because of Jehovah who is faithful, and the Holy One of Israel, and He chose You." (Isaiah 49: 6-7)

Jesus' mission – to restore the family of God and bring hundreds of thousands of Jews into a relationship with God – is too small! Because Jesus is obedient through this, God is now giving Him the entire world! "I will give You for a light of the nations, that You may be My salvation to the end of the earth." Jesus' faithfulness is the catalyst that expands His ministry beyond His imagination and goals.

God says this to "the despised of soul, to the hated of the nation," to Jesus in His darkest hour. God sees Jesus' distress and says He's not alone, that even in His darkest hour, there is hope and meaning.

"So says Jehovah, in a favorable time I have answered You, and in a day of salvation I have helped You. And I will preserve You and give You for a covenant of the people; to establish the earth, to cause to inherit the desolated inheritances; to say to the prisoners, 'Go out.' To those who are in darkness, 'Show yourselves!' They shall feed on the ways, and their pastures shall be in all high places. They shall not hunger nor thirst; and the heat and sun shall not strike them. For He who has mercy on them shall lead them; and He shall guide them by the springs of water. And I will make all My mountains a way, and My highways shall be set on high. Behold, these shall come from afar; and, lo, these from the north and from the west; and these from the land of Sinim." (Isaiah 49: 8-12)

God tells Jesus that all is not lost. In fact, here in Gethsemane, the fulfillment of His ministry is beginning. He calls this moment "a favorable time" and "a day of salvation." Jesus is sweating blood from the extreme stress of His emotions, and God answers with "Peace be with you. You can't see it, but You are going to save the whole world. People lost in sin, who have never heard of You or Me, are going to be saved from their darkness because of what You are doing right now."

Jesus understands the strength and everlastingness of God's word. Throughout His ministry, He watched as the spoken will of God created miracles all around Him. He knows that when God speaks, it is done.

Now these words of God are all Jesus has. The facts in front of Him do not line up with the promise God is giving. Yet, Jesus chose to stand on the faith God gave Him to believe His word, and He bore the torture of His death "for the joy [God] set before him" (Hebrews 12:2); the salvation of the world.

Jesus had to walk to the cross not knowing or seeing the fruit of His sacrifice but trusting only in God's promises for Him.

He had to because we have to.

This is Gethsemane. Jesus broken; a failure, throwing Himself on the ground before the Father, pleading for a second chance. Jesus blindly believing God's promises and obediently submitting to death. And God, our loving Father, so proud of His Son, so pleased that he has overcome this horrible temptation, gives Jesus everything! Lavishing His love on the Glory of His heart.

"Sing, O heavens; and be joyful, O earth; break out into singing, O mountains. For Jehovah has comforted His people and will have pity on His afflicted. But Zion said, 'Jehovah has forsaken me,' and 'My Lord has forgotten me.' Can a woman forget her suckling child, from pitying the son of her womb? Yea, these may forget, yet I will surely not forget you. Behold, I have carved you on the palms of My hands; your walls are ever before Me. Your sons hurry; those destroying you and ruining you shall go out from you. Lift up your eyes all around and see! They all gather and come to you. As I live, says Jehovah, you shall surely wear all of them as an ornament, and bind them on as a bride. For your wastes and your deserted places, and your land of ruins shall even now be too narrow to live there; and they who swallow you shall be broad. The sons of your bereavement shall yet say in your ears, 'The place is too narrow for me; come near so that I may live.' Then you shall say in your heart, 'Who has borne these to me, for I am bereaved and desolate, turned aside and an exile; who then has brought up these. Behold, I was left alone. Where do these come from'" (Isaiah 49: 13-21)

We all come to places in our lives where we say, "God doesn't care" or "I'm too bad for God to care for me."

Here is God's answer, "I cannot do anything but care for you. I cannot forget you. Just like a loving mother who cannot forget the needs of her child, I will never forget you. I see your pain. Do you see My love? Look around. I am removing all the people and things that have caused you pain and now they all return to you like beautiful jewels to wear that bring you joy! All your deserted places, your utter failures will be filled to overflowing with success and you will look around and say, how it happened when you were ruined and destitute? Where did all this come from?"

"So says the Lord Jehovah, Behold I will lift up My hand to the nations, and will set up My banner to peoples. And they shall bring your sons in the bosom, and your daughters shall be carried on the shoulder. And kings shall be your nursing fathers, and their queens your nurses. They shall bow to you, faces down to the earth, and lick up the dust of your feet. And you shall know that I am Jehovah, by whom they who wait for Me shall not be ashamed. Shall the booty be taken from the warrior, or the righteous captive escape? But so says Jehovah,

Even the captives of the warrior shall be taken, and the booty of the terrifying ones shall be delivered. For I will strive with him who contends with you; and I will save your sons. And those who oppress you, I will feed with their own flesh; and they shall be drunk by their own blood, as with fresh wind. And all flesh shall know that I, Jehovah, am your Savior and your Redeemer, the mighty One of Jacob. (Isaiah 49: 22-26)

Here is where it came from. God lifted His "hand to the nations" and "set up [His] banner to peoples," and they saw and came. This is Jesus on the cross, lifted for all to see. His "deserted place" became our greatest joy, bringing us to God. This ugly, horrific, blood-spattered wood is now a beautiful symbol of salvation across the world.

Before Jesus died for us, everyone ensnared by Satan was lost. Now "the captives of the warrior shall be taken, and the booty of the terrifying ones shall be delivered," because it is no longer we who fight for ourselves, but Jesus who fights in partnership with God and Holy Spirit to save us. The cross has transformed our captivity into freedom.

So now Jesus has been given not just the Jews, but the whole world. Those of us who are not in the ancestry of Israel are given the opportunity to become fully a member of God's family anyway. No more is our salvation about lineage, but about adoption. The power God gave Jesus in the cross is the power to make the unredeemable redeemed. His reward is the totality of a family bigger than He imagined.

"For I am not ashamed of the gospel of Christ, for it is the power of God to salvation for everyone who believes, for the Jew first and also for the Greek." (Romans 1:16)

When the facts of our life don't in any way look like the promises of God, we are called to walk blindly toward what God is calling us to do.

When Isaiah was called to blind faith

Isaiah faced the same decision "in the year Tartan came to Ash-dod." Will he blindly follow God's direction into humiliation or decide it's too much?

"In the year Tartan came to Ashdod, when Sargon the king of Assyria sent him, and fought against Ashdod, and took it; at that time Jehovah spoke by Isaiah the son of Amoz, saying, 'Go and loosen the sackcloth from your loins, and take your shoe off from your foot. And he did so, walking naked and barefoot. And Jehovah said, 'Just as My servant Isaiah has walked naked and barefoot three years – a sign and a wonder on Egypt and Ethiopia – so shall the king of Asyria lead away the captives of Egypt and the exiles of Ethiopia, young and old; naked and barefoot... And he who lives in this coast shall say in that day, 'Behold, this has become of our hope to which we fled for help there, to be delivered from before the king of Assyria;' and 'How shall we escape?'" (Isaiah 20)

At this time in Judah's history, they were afraid of Assyria's might and were seeking alliances with Egypt and Ethiopia, two other super-powers of the day. They had forgotten God and were putting all their hope in an earthly solution. If Judah was going to hear the Word of God and be saved from destruction, something drastic had to be done. No one was listening to Isaiah, so God asked him to do this extreme prophetic act to impact His people. Isaiah's nakedness was a graphic illustration of the sad future of Jerusalem's potential allies.

These verses make it seem so easy, but God was asking Isaiah to walk in absolute humiliation among the people. Not only would he lose any respect he had, but his family (he had a wife and two children) would also be subject to the same ridicule. That Isaiah endured this life for three years says something about the relationship he had with God, utter trust. It also testifies to how much he cared for Judah, that he would suffer their rebuke to make a point.

And Judah finally came to their senses. They stopped their negotiations with Egypt and Ethiopia and did not follow through with their political solution. They watched as Egypt and Ethiopia were conquered by Assyria and led into captivity in utter humiliation – naked and barefoot. Isaiah's humiliation suddenly became Judah's redemption.

It is so hard, and the temptation is to give up or go a different, easier way. But, just like Isaiah did for Israel, we have a Savior who embraced His humiliation to secure our redemption. We have an advocate, Jesus, who faced the very same temptations and trials we do and overcame them. We have a High Priest who stands before the Father praying for us, saying just the right words to bring God's blessing to us, because He has walked in our shoes and knows our anguish and tears, our "dark night of the soul."

When I was called to blind faith

My dark night of the soul was ending but driving across the country and that first year in Arizona was a fog. I worked in a convenience store as the night clerk. I lived with my parents because I couldn't think clearly enough to survive on my own. I wandered in and out of social events. I was lost, but God is faithful.

My sister invited me to her church, and I found a home there in her church family. God drew me closer to Himself during worship times and prayer. I continued to read the Bible and Barclay because they had worked for me before, but God eventually drew me away from former things and showed me new ways to study and pray. I read the Bible from cover to cover, and then I did it again. The Chronological Bible fascinated me, a Bible arranged completely in chronological order, the psalms David wrote are inserted in Kings and Chronicles where the events happened. The gospels are mixed together and give a complete picture of Jesus' life. It's not a Bible where you can find scripture references easily, but overall, it's a wonderful read. Slowly God was bringing me into a new walk of trust and blind faith.

One morning I was thinking about my 30th birthday coming up. It seemed such a turning point, and I thought I should plan my life a bit better. Something didn't quite feel right about that birthday, and when I did the math, I realized I was going to be 31! I had lost a year!! That was a wake-up call to me to get my act together. I had to pull myself out of this fog and begin to live again.

I determined that this was a second chance at life. My son and I were all the way across the country where no one knew us. I could re-create myself anyway I wanted. I turned to God, rebuilding my world around His Word.

I began dating a man who had a good heart. He was actually kind to me, and I was happy, but sex was a big part of our relationship. God used that to convict me and teach me that maybe romantic love could be found without physical passion. When my boyfriend migrated to Massachusetts, we kept in touch, writing and talking on the phone, but when I told him I had been convicted about sex and would not continue that part of our relationship, he couldn't understand and thought I was rejecting him. He found another girlfriend, and that was that. I was hurt, but not broken. God was calling me, and this time I was listening.

This new life of celibacy was challenging, but I would not relent. God was teaching me to understand love in a completely new way. I did not understand, but now I knew what *not* to do!

After a year with my parents, I finally got an apartment and a job substitute teaching. Between that, a job as a Church Choir Director, and supplies as a local food bank, my son and I got by. I had been a successful teacher, married to a successful teacher, living in a nice house, and wanting for nothing. Now I was scraping by on fumes, grateful for the welfare state, counting every penny and hoping the food bank had "good stuff" this week.

It seemed like God was peeling away everything I knew as true. I was blind to my future. Every job I tried ended quickly. Things I had succeeded with before seemed to melt away before they could be established: Jobs in sales, office administration, teaching, singing, development, nothing "stuck" except my very part-time job as a choir director in a small Episcopalian Church.

But God was doing something. My prayer life was being transformed. Estranged in a house that discouraged relationship, my sister and I had never really been sisters, but now we were getting closer and becoming the sisters I had always dreamed of. The church I was attending reminded me of the barn in the woods back in college, and I could feel my soul resting in the healing balm of God's love. Everything that was important had shifted away from the "American dream" and into a deeper bond with Jesus.

"Ho, everyone who thirsts, come to the water; and he who has no money, come buy grain and eat. Yes, come buy grain, wine and milk without silver and with no price. . .Bend your ear and come to Me; hear and your soul shall live; and I will cut a covenant everlasting with you. . .Seek Jehovah while He may be found; call on Him while He is near. Let the wicked forsake his way and the vain man his thoughts; and let him return to Jehovah, and He will have mercy on him – and to our God, for He will abundantly pardon." (Isaiah 55:1-7)

This was where I was, drinking deeply of the waters with nothing to give. Eating from His table with nothing to offer Him. Yet, He gave and gave and had mercy on me.

Life was not without its challenges, but my heart was now tied to God and I was not going to turn away again. The price was too high. I gladly walked blindly into this new future, knowing only the goodness of God and trusting in His love for me. Isaiah had done it. Jesus had done it. Now He would help me do it, too.

"Unless the Lord builds the house, they labor in vain who build it." (Psalm 127:1)

God will build, or we will fail. And when God builds, it is joy to bend into His construction. This is a lesson worth learning.

DIGGING DEEPER

- **Read Hebrews 2: 17-18**. Rewrite it in your own words. (How would you say it to someone else if you didn't have your Bible with you?)

- What was God's reaction to Jesus' blind trust in Him? Do you think God feels the same way about you? Explain.

- Have you ever reached a point of blind faith; a Gethsemane moment? What happened? What did God do?

- Think of three reasons to praise God right now.

Understanding through intimacy

"No longer do I call you servants for a servant does not know what his master is doing, but I have called you friends, for all things that I heard from My Father I have made known to you." (John 15:15)

I love Isaiah 30 and 31.

Isaiah obeyed God to his own detriment. Why? Because he knew the heart of God and loved His people. Isaiah knew God's nature, heard what He was saying, and trusted His word. It's like they sat on the back-porch spending time together as friends do. It's a brilliant example of how friendship with God works. We yield to the love of God, and He grows our relationship. Isaiah, me, you, we *all* can have this.

"Now come, write it before them on a tablet, and note it on a book, so that it may be for the latter day, until forever." (Isaiah 30:8)

So God says, "Come over here, Isaiah, and write this down. These people don't get it like you and I do. I know you understand what I'm trying to say, so I'd like you to make a permanent record. Then, after you die and they come to their senses, they will read it and understand Me."

"Jehovah has said to me; As the lion roars, even the young lion on his prey when the multitude of shepherds are gathered against him, he will not fear their voice, nor

75

fret himself because of their noise. So Jehovah of hosts will shield over Jerusalem, shielding and delivering, and passing over, He will save it." (Isaiah 31:4-5)

And Isaiah says, "Listen to me, Jerusalem! God and I have had a talk, and He confided in me that you guys are going to be OK. I know Him. He's like a great and fierce lion who isn't afraid of a few shepherds. So, when enemies come against you, know that this great and fierce lion is not bothered or intimidated by a few armies. He'll protect you and send them packing! He's like that. He enjoys protecting you."

"Thorns and briars shall spring up on the land of My people, even over all the houses of joy in the jubilant city, because the palace is forsaken; the crowd of the city is forsaken, mound and tower are instead caves, until forever; a joy of wild asses; pasture for flocks; until is poured out on us the Spirit from on high, and the wilderness becomes a fruitful field; and the fruitful field is reckoned as a forest. Then justice shall dwell in the wilderness, and righteousness shall dwell in the fruitful field. And the work of righteousness shall be peace; and the service of righteousness shall be quietness and hope forever." (Isaiah 32:13-17)

"Things are looking bad for us, but my Friend is coming and when He gets here – Wow – there's going to be big changes. He'll make the crops grow, spread joy all around, and bring peace and justice to everyone forever. I know this because I know Him. Trust me, He won't disappoint."

"Behold, Zion, the city of our appointed meeting! Your eyes shall see Jerusalem, a quiet home, a tent that shall not be moved; its stakes shall not be pulled up forever, nor shall any of its cords be pulled off. But majestic Jehovah will place there for us a place of rivers and streams, broad on both hand; a ship with oars shall not go in it, and a majestic boat shall not pass through it. For Jehovah is our judge; Jehovah is our lawgiver; Jehovah is our king; He will save us." (Isaiah 33:20-22)

When you stand before a beautiful house for the first time, can you describe the inside before you go in? Of course not! This detailed description of a new Zion is proof that Isaiah had been to "God's house," deep into His presence. That's what friends do, visit each other at home. And now Isaiah is saying, "I want you to imagine what I've seen. This wonderful place of peace and goodness. It's going to be ours; just come with me and worship God." God took His friend to His house, and it is glorious!

God invites us into this friendship, too. He was wooing me into it, and as I slowly walked forward into His will, I began to change.

I never really understood what being a seer meant. I just saw stuff and didn't know what it was. Angels, demons, they all looked the same – beings that frightened me because they were not of earth. I was extremely scared of the dark when I was a child; that was when these things revealed themselves. Even as an adult the darkness made me uncomfortable, sometimes frightened, because I knew there was something out there even if I couldn't see it.

I never told anyone about this. I thought it was a little insanity. But God wanted to teach me about Himself and His world. Now in a culture of miracles among searchers for the Holy Spirit, I realized it was spiritual revelations and I began to be open about it.

My sister was my confidant. She took all my revelations in stride, explaining that she, too, had this gift and taught me what she knew about it. We began to share visions and dreams, pondering the awesomeness of God. I began to experience things I had never imagined.

Oh, He was pouring into me! Visions, dreams, prophecies, words of knowledge, I didn't know what half of it was, but I was walking in the glory of the Lord! I held all these experiences in my heart, lifted by the inspiration of them all. I was learning about God in new and glorious ways. He was revealing Himself, becoming my Friend and I was loving it!

Worship would bring joy and peace. I knew He was healing me, and I felt contentment for the first time in my life. No pain of revelation. No shame of exposed sin. Just real contentment. Every encounter with Him was full of love. I wanted it to go on forever, but God is never stagnant, and He wanted more from me. I was determined to stay in experience, and He wanted friendship.

"The whole vision to you is like the words of a sealed book which they give to one knowing books saying, 'Please read this.' Then he says, 'I am not able, for it is sealed.' And the book is given to one who does not know books, saying, 'Please read this.' Then he says, 'I do not know books." (Isaiah 29:11-12)

We are called to understand what we read in scripture. We are instructed to pray into words and revelations given to us. But many of us see "the seal," awed by the majesty of God and the mystery of it all, and say, "Oh, I can't break this. Let's just look at the outside." Or we believe we're not qualified and say, "I don't know anything about that, and I'm not able to learn."

God's urging for me to learn to interpret these visions rather than just experience them was becoming stronger. I began to pray, study, and learn how to do that. It soon became evident that there was a responsibility to deliver the words given to us, and I began to speak out to the church at large. Although the people around me didn't seem to judge me, they didn't know what to do with me either. I was relishing the experience of delivering these words, never thinking that there might be consequences I didn't like.

I had always been a preformer and taken pride in my talents. That pride wrapped in performance was still there. I kept God's glory for myself. "Look at me! God has given me something for you. That makes me special and holy." I thought they would appreciate me, but this was more than they bargained for. Without moving into deeper intimacy with God a chance to grow in Him was transformed into a chance to glorify myself.

The gifts of healing and prophecy were also showing themselves through me. I liked prophecy; it made me feel powerful and in control. I could tell someone about themselves and amaze them. Healing, on the other hand, required risk. I prayed, and God decided whether to heal or not. This was not comfortable for me because I perceived a "non-healing in the moment prayer" as a failure. Failure was something I still couldn't deal with because it made me look weak. My value was in what others thought of me, not what God thought of me.

This "fear of man" eventually drove me to hold back and not pray or release what God was showing me. People seemed to be thinking I was strange, and that hurt me too much. God was after my total health, but I was manipulated by my fear. He continued to pour His Spirit into me, but now I was resisting.

"Say to those who are fearful-hearted, 'Be strong, do not fear! Behold, your God will come with vengeance, with the recompense of God. He will come and save you.' Then the eyes of the blind shall be opened, and the ears of the deaf shall be unstopped. Then the lame shall leap like a deer, and the tongue of the dumb sing. For waters shall burst forth in the wilderness, and streams in the desert. The parched ground shall become a pool, and the thirsty land springs of water; in the habitation of jackals, where each lay, there shall be grass with reeds and rushes." (Isaiah 35:4-7)

This is what the gifts of the Holy Spirit are for – the blessing of others. God comes and reveals Himself through miracles: opening blind eyes and deaf ears, restoring lame limbs, and giving speech back to those who can't talk. These are the "waters" bursting forth in the wilderness of lives without God. These are the streams in the deserts of loneliness and heartache. God comes to save and His gifts in us are for releasing His presence on the earth and its people.

Visions, words of knowledge, urges to heal and pray, are to

be released. Our job is to deliver. God will move in the delivery whether we see it or not. That is not for us to worry about. We are to receive, release, and minister, and then walk away until God gives more direction. I was having a hard time with that.

"Now come, write it before them on a tablet, and note it on a book, so that it may be for the latter day, until forever, that this is a rebellious people, lying sons; sons who are not willing to hear the law of Jehovah; who say to the seers, 'Do not see;' and to the visioners, 'Do not have a vision for right things to us; speak smooth things to us, have a vision of trifles. Turn aside from the way; stretch from the path; cause the Holy One of Israel to cease from before us.' (Isaiah 30:8-10)

This word given to Isaiah was not for the enemies of Israel, but for the children of God. God was using His prophets and seers to talk to His children, but, just like me, they didn't want to hear what He had to say. God's words weren't easy, He was calling them out of their lives of sin and neglect and back to Himself. They didn't like it, so they closed their ears and minds to anything that didn't fit the pretty words and easy life they wanted.

That is just what I was doing. God was revealing wonderful things to me, but some hard words, too. He was showing me illness and sin in others He wanted me to pray for. He was asking me to talk to strangers about their lives. He was trying to move through me to touch others, and I was afraid. I found myself asking Him for only the positive words, only the pretty visions, and nice dreams. I wanted unicorns and fairy dust, and He was giving me reality.

"Take heed to yourselves, lest you forget the covenant of the Lord your God which He made with you, and make for yourselves a carved image in the form of anything which the Lord your God has forbidden you. For the Lord your God is a consuming fire, a jealous God."
(Deuteronomy 4:23-24)

My "carved image" was the firm belief that God's words would always be positive, causing the other person to smile and appreciate everything I had said. I worshipped that belief, clinging to it so hard that I believed words of truth that were hard to bear must be from the devil. When God required me to move into someone's life with a word that was difficult, I counted it as evil and resisted with all my being. Fear will do that; consume you and twist the gifts and revelations of God into some wretched thing you can't recognize.

I was paralyzed. Eventually, moving out in faith to pray was out of the question. I was counting my fear of failure as words of wisdom, and I refused to release what God was so graciously giving me. Urges to pray for others in the moment became stronger and stronger until they were a burden, but I still wouldn't do it. Prophetic words I never gave filled my mind to distraction, taking over my thoughts. But still I kept it all in, my unwillingness to deliver stacking burden on burden and heartache on heartache until I couldn't stand it anymore. "Please, take this from me!" was my soul's cry.

And, suddenly it was gone.

I was relieved at first. The oppression and pain were gone. But I quickly realized that so was God's immediate presence and His voice. So were dreams and visions and prophetic words and everything I knew God to be in my life. I knew He hadn't abandoned me, but the connection I had held so dear had disappeared. I found myself regretting my decision, made from myself and not directed by Him. My pleas to Him to return went unanswered.

I was in a wilderness of my own making, and it took 20 years to find my way out.

DIGGING DEEPER

- **Read Isaiah 35: 4-7.** Consider the list of things that will happen when God comes "with vengeance" (lame walk, blind see, etc.). Who do you think He's taking vengeance on?

- **Read Isaiah 30: 8-10.** How is this manifesting in God's people today? How is society negatively impacting your life? Influencing you to lean away from God?

- **Read Deut. 4: 23-24.** What do the words "consuming fire" and "jealous God" tell you about God's love for you?

Understanding Through repentance

"Then as [Jesus] entered a certain village, there met Him ten men who were lepers, who stood afar off. And they lifted up their voices and said, "Jesus, Master, have mercy on us!"

So when He saw them, He said to them, "Go show yourselves to the priests." And so it was that as they went, they were cleansed. And one of them, when he saw that he was healed, returned, and with a loud voice glorified God, and fell down on his face at His feet, giving Him thanks. And he was a Samaritan. So Jesus answered and said, "Were there not ten cleansed? But where are the nine? Were there not any found who returned to give glory to God except this foreigner? And He said to him, "Arise, go your way. Your faith has made you well." (Luke 17:12-19)

Jesus healed all 10 lepers of leprosy, but only one came back to worship Him. Their miraculous healing was a sign of the glory of the kingdom of God, and only 1 of the 10 understood this. His heart drove him back to humbly worship at the feet of Jesus and declare his unworthiness and gratitude. Because he did this act of repentance, Jesus gave him a deeper healing. The Greek word for healing used in the phrase "Your faith has made you well" is "sozo." Strong's Exhaustive Concordance defines it "to deliver, heal, save, be made whole." Clearly, this man received more healing than his friends. They were all physically healed, but this man was also given deliverance. He was "made whole" and saved. He was healed of *everything*, straight down through his soul.

Just like the 10 lepers, we can receive healing and the joy of the Lord, but there is a deeper healing, a "wholeness" to be gained through humbling ourselves in repentance. It has always been so with God.

The danger is in receiving the healing and not desiring the intimacy. Isaiah 38 and 39 tells this story clearly; a lesson we all need to learn.

The story begins with Hezekiah's battle with sickness. He has an ulcer that has apparently gone septic. He's bedridden and in great pain. He sends for Isaiah to see if there's anything the man of God can do for him, but all Isaiah says is, "Yep, you're gonna die," and then he walks out.

Hezekiah turns over to the wall and cries. He prays to God for mercy, and before Isaiah leaves the castle, God tells him to go back, and He gives him the cure for Hezekiah. To prove to Hezekiah that He will fulfill His promise, God moves the sun back in the sky to start the day over. Hezekiah recovers and is amazed at what happens next.

When God moved the sun back in the sky, the whole world experienced it! When kings found out it was tied to a miracle for Hezekiah, they began to send him gifts; very valuable gifts: gold, silver, fine cloth, spices, things that filled Hezekiah's treasury to the brim and made him a very rich and influential man.

All this went to his head. He didn't honor God or humble himself before Him as he should have. Instead, he became very pleased with his new status and proud to tell anyone about it. He was full of self-centered importance and convinced that everyone thought he was as remarkable as he thought he was.

When the prince of Babylon arrived with even more treasures, Hezekiah couldn't help but brag. Those gifts just kept coming, and he was giddy with the attention. He showed the prince everything, held nothing back. He knew nothing about the Babylonians, how ruthless they were, and how greedy for more. His pride and arrogance made Judah vulnerable to a very big and strong kingdom that now set its sights on Israel's booty.

God sent Isaiah back to the king to deliver a message. When Babylon returns, they will be merciless. They're not interested in tribute; they want everything and everyone and will not settle for less. Even Hezekiah's family will be taken. His sons will be castrated and made to serve in the king's palace.

And here is the evidence of Hezekiah's self-centeredness. When he is told that his family and his country will not survive, he is relieved that it will happen to his sons, but not to him. He shall live in peace and not have to reap the consequences of his actions. His concern is not for the future of his family, but for his own comfort.

God has shown him miraculous love and healing in answer to his prayer. On the verge of death, he was given life. On the verge of bankruptcy, he was restored richer than before. Hezekiah doesn't seem to be able to put this together. He cries out to God for mercy when <u>his</u> life is on the line, but when it is the lives of his sons and his country, well... not so much.

He could have cried out to God again for his people and expected the same miraculous answer of deliverance. He was the king. It was his job to intercede for Israel. God had shown Hezekiah in a huge way that He listened to his prayers. God had also shown him that the words delivered by Isaiah could be changed. Hezekiah <u>chose</u> not to save his people.

God was ready to act. He had shown Himself ready to save, and Hezekiah did nothing – NOTHING! He was so lost in his own comfort it didn't occur to him to cry out for Israel, and the result was a catastrophe, an exile like they had never experienced before. After Hezekiah's death, the Babylonians returned, carrying off the nation into brutal slavery.

I'm not proud of it, but I was in the same boat as Hezekiah. My pride in "my" skill as a seer was my downfall. I had shown everyone my gift and received all the glory for it. Because I clung to it for myself, it became too much to hold and I lost everything. Now I was in spiritual exile.

I turned to the only tool left to me, my Bible. I had been

studying and teaching the Bible for many years, so it was an old friend to me. I began to read it cover to cover again and again, finding its rhythm and flow. I prayed in tongues, hoping this spiritual language would reconnect me with all I had before. But God was changing me and waiting. . .

"For the weapons of our warfare are not carnal but mighty in God for pulling down strongholds, casting down arguments and every high thing that exalts itself against the knowledge of God, bringing every thought into captivity to the obedience of Christ, and being ready to punish all disobedience when our obedience is fulfilled." (2 Corinthians 10:4-6)

I had proven myself untrustworthy, and now I had to regain His trust. This is not easy with a God who can see right into your heart and know your hidden fears and motivations. He began to "clean me up" and remake this vessel.

I thought I could work my way back into His good graces. That didn't go well, but I tried none-the-less. Everything I did, I did in my own strength, and so it got me nothing. I read a gazillion books and became known as the "go-to" with questions about theology. I studied the Bible every day. I began to preach in that little Episcopalian church. I behaved and talked with "holiness" and wore beautiful, big crosses to church.

I really don't know what I was thinking. The pride and fear in me were twisting everything. I thought I was humble and caring, but it was just self-serving shows of kindness and knowledge. I wasn't progressing in faith at all, just wallowing around in the same mud-patch thinking it's nirvana.

Several years into this, I met and fell in love with a man who fell in love with me. He wasn't a Christian, but I was so passionate about him I didn't care. This powerful love frightened me. I prayed to God to take this love from me if he wasn't the man I was to marry. The love just got stronger. I was convinced that God was giving me His blessing.

We married and began a new life together. My son was 8; my

husband was a teacher; we lived in a beautiful house – I felt my life was finally on track.

But after a few years, the marriage got difficult. My husband didn't appreciate my son's strong will and, like me, when challenged, my son would dig in his heels. The tension between them built to dangerous levels.

I also was the brunt of the sting of my husband's sarcastic humor which built walls in me against him. I was not blameless. I loved him but could not open my emotional self to be vulnerable to him, and he sensed this. From the start, there was a distance between us that was all on me. All this kept building and building until, after 10 years, he left and eventually divorced me.

I was devastated. I was very ashamed of being twice divorced. It seemed a very unholy state to be in. I found it hard to tell people that. I was still wrapped up in their opinions defining me.

For a year and a half, I wandered around, trying to piece my life back together. He had moved only a few miles away, and I longed for him to come back to me. Even with my defenses, I loved him more than I had ever loved any man, and I missed him terribly.

One day I was walking in the living room, and my grief suddenly overcame me. I fell to my knees and cried out to God. "Why? Why did You tell me to marry him if it all came to this?"

Then, finally, I heard His voice. It had been so many years since He had come so near to me, I had despaired of ever having this joy again. He said, "You have learned all you can from him. It's time to move on."

I was shocked. Marriage was a sacred thing. This couldn't be God! I began to look up scriptures about marriage to prove that this word was not His and then I found this:

"A woman who has a husband who does not believe, if he is willing to live with her, let her not divorce him.... But if the unbeliever departs, let him depart, a brother or a sister is not under bondage in such cases." (1 Corinthians 7:13-15)

That is exactly what had happened! When he asked me for a divorce, I said, "If that's what you want, I won't fight you, but I won't help you." Without knowing it, I had done the Biblical thing! You'd think this would be cause for celebration, but it threw me into reflection and prayer. I had been absolved of this "sin" of divorce, but now what? How had this happened again? What was it in me that kept bringing me to this place?

Now I was ready. God began by showing me what I had learned in this marriage:

- I had learned what naked truth was and that it was good to walk in. My husband was insistent that we talk things out. Dancing around the truth must go in the current of these conversations. Speaking plainly and clearly was something I had never done before.
- He had taught me how to move comfortably in groups of people who had nothing in common with me. The last few years of our marriage my husband adopted the New Age lifestyle. We attended functions and workshops together; he was happy – I was mightily resistant. God revealed the lies and absurdities to me, and I began to learn spiritual warfare in the middle of the enemy's camp.
- I learned just how much I was driven by emotions and feelings I didn't understand. My defenses got in the way of our relationship. I became aware of this because I *wanted* to love him more. I certainly felt more love than I was showing, but try as I might, I just couldn't do any more than I was, and it wasn't enough.
- God had taught me to love people who didn't love me. These new-age people sensed my resistance and began to ignore me in favor of my husband, who seemed receptive. They had no love for anyone who didn't appreciate them. God gave me compassion to pray and forgive. I began to see even my husband in a different light; illuminated from God's perspective.

These revelations drove me into an attitude of thankfulness for all this marriage had brought me and opened me to a time of repentance and healing.

This was not the "I dedicate everything to God" fervor that was mine in college. It wasn't a craving for more experiences of God either. Now I was serious and calm, moving into God with slow determination. Every step was measured and prayed about. I knew this path would determine my future and I wanted God firmly planted in it. I counted the cost: the loss of everything I knew, the blind trust necessary to move forward, turning again into the pains that still lingered in my soul and exposing them to God's healing, accepting His joy as my strength and not walking in my own.

He showed me the pains of my youth and healed me. I gave him my sins, and He forgave me. He revealed lies I had believed all my life, and I gave them up. I gave Him permission to dig deeper, and He gently moved like an archeologist to reveal my worthless potsherds and His beautiful treasures.

> "Comfort, O comfort My people," says your God. "Speak lovingly to the heart of Jerusalem – yes, cry to her that her warfare is done, that her iniquity is pardoned; for she has taken from the hand of Jehovah double for all her sins. The voice of him who cries in the wilderness: "Prepare the way of Jehovah; make straight in the desert a highway for our God. Every valley shall be exalted, and every mountain and hill shall be made low and the knoll shall be a level place, and the rough places a plain. And the glory of Jehovah shall be revealed, and all flesh shall see it together, for the mouth of Jehovah has spoken." (Isaiah 40:1-5)

My God was comforting me, speaking lovingly to me, bringing me out from the pain of my life into a new relationship with Him that was full of peace and joy. For nearly 50 years, I had fought against the world and God to preserve myself. Now, exposed and vulnerable, He was building me into the woman I was always meant to be.

Everything I had struggled to hold on to had to be given up. Every sin I had justified had to be repented of. Every time I did that, a piece of me would be lost, and a new part of Him would replace it. The God I understood was too small. He was so much bigger than my mind could imagine. There was to be nothing but Him, that frightened me, and yet everything I had ever wanted or longed for began to be revealed in His presence. He truly is everything we desire.

> "Who has measured in His palm the waters and the heavens by a span meted out; and enclosed in the measure the dust of the earth, and weighed in the balance the mountains, and the hills in the scales? Who has meted out the Spirit of Jehovah, or a man His counsel taught Him? With whom did He take counsel, and who trained Him and taught Him in the path of justice; and taught Him knowledge, and made known to Him the way of discernment? (Isaiah 40: 12-14)

How great is God? He is the answer to all these questions. He knows exactly how much water is on the earth and can tell us exactly how much volume there is in space. He knows every dust particle and their accumulated weight, even the measure of mountains. The Spirit of God is greater than any man can even imagine. He knows everything; there is nothing anyone can tell Him He doesn't already know. All the things of the earth that are so grand to us are just little things to Him. He is beyond our wildest imagination.

Such a great and powerful God is so easily perceived as judgmental and terrible in power. But He calls us to see Him differently. He points to the universe that proves His creative power and helps us to see His glory and His strength. He tells us that He knows our deepest secrets and secret doings. That should scare us. It is too vulnerable a thing to be scrutinized by someone who knows <u>everything</u> about you.

And yet He says "Come out of your fears and see that I am your Savior. I never get tired and I understand everything without having to think about it. All the power I used to create the universe I will use to help you. There is nothing you can hide from Me. I know all your weaknesses. So, when you are weak, I will be your never-failing strength. In places where you have never been strong, I will put My strength in you. Young men are the go-to guys when lots of strength is needed, but even they have their limits. My strength is for everyone and never fails." (paraphrase of Isaiah 40:9-13)

This is the creator of all things showing us His love; telling us that He will use all His strength and might to help us. He will give to us the fullness of who He is to keep us strong. His breath will not destroy us, but restore us with the gentle, life-giving breath of His Holy Spirit.

> "Be quiet before Me, O coasts; and let peoples renew their power." (Isaiah 41:1)

"Be quiet before Me." In the stillness of His presence is refreshing and renewal. Just invite Him to be with you and wait, knowing that He is faithful. This is the secret to unimaginable peace and confidence in faith; it is Jesus' gift to us in His presence. It is a connection to God's heart.

There is no clearer illustration of this than Isaiah. Hearing God's heart, he says to the people,

> "And to whom will you liken God? Or what likeness will you array to Him? ... Have you not known? Have you not heard? Was it not told to you from the beginning? ... He who stretches the heavens like a curtain and spreads them like a tent to live in; who gives potentates into nothing – He makes judges of the earth as nothing." (Isaiah 40: 18-23)

And then God says to the people,

> "And to whom will you liken Me, or am I equaled" says the Holy One? "Lift up your eyes on high and see: Who has created these, bringing out their host by number? By greatness of vigor and might of power He calls them all by name and not one is lacking." (Isaiah 40:25-26)

Are they not saying the same thing? Two hearts beating in time with each other. Isaiah has journeyed through rules, experience, blind faith, repentance, and friendship to live in God's heart. His intimacy with God blesses us with insights into His nature and words of love for His people.

DIGGING DEEPER

- What does the story of Hezekiah tell us about ourselves?

- Why do you think Hezekiah chose not to pray for his people?

- **Read Isaiah 40: 12-14**. What do these questions tell you about God? About yourself?

- **Read Isaiah 41:1**. Spend at least 10 minutes right now being quiet and thinking about the goodness of God. Invite Him to be present and touch you.

- What did you experience in those moments? Did God reveal anything to you?

Father, Son and Holy Spirit in their own words. . .

"This is He who came by water and blood – Jesus Christ, not only by water, but by water and blood. And it is the Spirit who bears witness, because the Spirit is truth. For there are three that bear witness in heaven; the Father, the Word, and the Holy Spirit, and these three are one." (1 John 5: 6-7)

Please indulge me as we step back and admire God once again. Jesus, Father, and Holy Spirit long to reveal themselves to us. When we connect to the heart of God, suddenly we can begin to understand His nature.

Isaiah, chapter 50 is a rare and special place in the Bible. The saving power of God is revealed through each voice of the Trinity. They show us a glimpse of their relationship to each other and the love and redeeming power that saves us from ourselves.

First the Father speaks –

"So says Jehovah, Where is the scroll of your mother's divorce whom I have put away? Or who of My creditors that I have sold you to him? Behold, you were sold for your iniquities, and your mother was put away for your trespasses. Who knows why I have come, and no one is here? I called, and not one answered. Is My hand truly cut short from ransom?: Or is there not power in Me to deliver? Behold, at My rebuke I dry up the sea, I make rivers a wilderness; their fish stink because of no water, and die in thirst. I clothe the heavens with blackness, and sackcloth sets their covering" (Isaiah 50: 1-3)

"Was it Me who left you or you who left Me?" God doesn't divorce us or sell us away. *We choose to walk away.* He is God, the Creator God. The whole universe and eternity exist because He wants it so. This power is His to wield, and we are helpless in the face of it.

But all the displays of His power are only to show us the greatness of His love for us and His ability to save us. There is nothing that can stop Him from redeeming His children. Even the darkness is by His design, showing His glory by contrast. He is ever near, calling us back to Himself.

Now Jesus speaks —
"The Lord Jehovah has given to Me the tongue of taught ones, to know, to help the weary with a word. He arouses in the morning; He arouses the ear to Me, to hear as the learned. The Lord Jehovah has opened My ear and I did not rebel; I did not turn away backwards. I gave My back to strikers, and My cheeks to pluckers; I did not hide My face from shame and spitting. And the Lord Jehovah will help Me. On account of this I was not ashamed. On account of this I set My face like flint, and I know that I shall not be ashamed. My Justifier is near. Who will contend with me? Let us stand up together, who is master of My judgment? Let him come near to Me. Behold, the Lord Jehovah will help Me; who is the one who will condemn Me? Behold, like a garment they shall wear out; the moth shall eat them."
(Isaiah 50: 4-10)

Jesus carried the wisdom of God to such a degree that people with receptive hearts could not deny that He was divine. His trust in God was so great that He allowed Himself to be whipped, beaten, and spit upon, knowing it was God's will that it be so. This is the faith of a man in His darkest moment. He knows the pain He will face and, with nothing but the promises of His Father, He steeled Himself to endure. "I did not hide My face from shame and spitting" all the way to the cross.

And because His faith was unwavering, He now stands and invites anyone who dares to contend with Him. "Behold, like a garment they shall wear out; the moth shall eat them." His enemies will die and disappear. Yet, He will be with the Father, who justifies Him and glorifies Him at His right hand.

Jesus, who died and rose again for us, is the right hand of God, glorified forever – "The Lamb of God who takes away the sin of the world." (John 1:29)

Now the Holy Spirit –

"Who among you fears Jehovah, obeying the voice of His servant, who walks in darkness, and no light is in him? Let him trust in the name of Jehovah, and lean on his God. Behold, all of you who kindle fire, who are encircled by sparks; walk in the light of your fire and in the sparks you are burning. This shall be to you from My hand; you shall lie down in pain. (Isaiah 50: 10-11)

Ever the teacher, Holy Spirit is the voice of God in our hearts and minds. He is devoted to glorifying Jesus and this is no exception. "Who among you fears Jehovah, obeying the voice of His servant?" Holy Spirit calls us to faithfulness and shines His light on Jesus.

In this case, the people are not listening, worshipping other gods with fire and spectacle. So, in this case, Holy Spirit is taking the people to the woodshed for some Holy discipline. The worship experience they have created will become the very thing that "burns" them. He will not allow God and Jesus to be maligned by idolatrous services.

God the Father, loves and calls to us. Jesus sacrificed Himself so that we could hear the Father's call and answer. Holy Spirit guides and directs those who give their lives to Jesus and works to bring those who are chosen into relationship. He keeps our eyes on holiness and teaches us about our triune God.

Here is love manifested for us. Here is the God we worship made clear through each voice of His three aspects. Father, Son, and Holy Spirit are our God, working together for our benefit; moving heaven and earth to love us.

DIGGING DEEPER

- What has God revealed to you about the nature of the Trinity?

- If God is calling us back to Himself, how does Jesus fit into that?

- What is the Holy Spirit's role in our lives? How is He different than God and Jesus?

- How do you feel about the Triune God working constantly for you? Why would they do that?

Understanding through His heart

"Blessed are the pure in heart, for they shall see God."
(Matthew 5:8)

Although the entire Bible is about God's love for us, Isaiah 45 gives us a glimpse of the depth of that love. He tells us about God's heart as He reveals it to God's people, a heart that never changes and loves us today like He loved then.

Cyrus worshipped the pagan gods of Persia. He didn't really know of God except by the Israelites' worship of Him. Yet, God chose him to free His people. He made him such a strong military might that Persia under his rule covered almost all the known world! This is supernatural stuff! God did this to show Himself to Cyrus; even Cyrus couldn't take credit for the magnitude of his victories. Kings brought treasures to him that had been kept in secret. Cities fell before him like melted butter.

Why would God do this for a pagan king? "For My servant Jacob's sake, and for Israel, My chosen, I even call you by your name. I name you, but you do not know Me" (Isaiah 45:4) To God, it doesn't matter that Cyrus has no faith in Him, has no knowledge even of His existence. God's children were going to go back to Israel and God used Cyrus to do it. He will manipulate His creation to bring about His intended eternal purpose. God's zealous love for His children drives Him to stop at nothing to bless and care for them.

"Drop down from above, O heavens; and let the cloud pour down righteousness. Let the earth open and let salvation bear fruit; and in righteousness sprout together

– I, Jehovah, have created it." (Isaiah 45:8)

His blessings fill the earth and the earth receives them and flourishes. The earth does not question God's motivations. It just receives all that He gives and uses it to the fullest. If we do the same; open ourselves to a loving God and trust Him to care for us, then our salvation will bear fruit, and all God's people who seek after His righteousness will grow together in His blessing. This is what God creates for us.

"To whom will you compare Me and make Me equal; and compare Me that we may be alike?. . .Remember former things from forever, for I am God, and no one else is God, even none like Me, declaring the end from the beginning, and from the past those things which were not done, saying, 'My purpose shall rise;' and 'I will do all My desire;' calling a bird of prey from the sunrise, the man of My counsel from a far off land. Yes, I have spoken; yes, I will cause it to come; I have formed; yes, I will do it. (Isaiah 46: 5-11)

There is no other god or religion like God. There just isn't. In the world of "other gods," there are two schools of thought; you must earn your way into heaven with a good life, or you can live any way you choose because we all are going to heaven (or a "universal consciousness") when we die. The first places all the consequences of the world's actions squarely on your shoulders ("this bad thing happened because *you* did something bad" – karma if you will) and the second is amoral; "any consequences I have to face are unfair; nothing's my fault."

They are both completely self-centered. There is no love in them, even though some are couched in terms of brotherhood and tolerance. God is no comparison.

He speaks and life comes into being. He calls and the response appears from places we never knew existed. He is outside time "declaring the end from the beginning." He speaks into the world and events line up to bring about the very things He spoke. This is the God we worship; the God who loves us.

"Listen to Me, mighty ones of heart who are far from righteousness; I bring near My righteousness; it shall not be far off, and My salvation shall not wait; I will place salvation in Zion, My glory for Israel." (Isaiah 46: 12-13)

"You strong, stalwart people who do not know Me, listen to Me. I will come right into your camp. I will show Myself to you in glory and when you fall on your face in fear, I will raise you up, forgive your sins, and bring you into My family. My salvation for you will be swift and complete, open to all who hear. This is the manifestation of My glory."

God will not leave the world lost in their own devices and burdens, our manufactured belief systems. He will come into the midst of us and be totally accessible to save.

DIGGING DEEPER

- **Read Isaiah 45:8**. How does God use nature to teach us about Himself?

- **Read Isaiah 46: 5-11.** List all the ways this scripture shows us God's love.

- **Read Isaiah 46:12-13.** How does Jesus fulfill this scripture? How does He continue to fulfill it throughout your life?

Understanding
Through our change of heart

"Therefore, submit to God, Resist the devil and he will flee from you. Draw near to God and He will draw near to you. Cleanse your hands, you sinners, and purify your hearts, you double-minded." (James 4:7-8)

"Meanwhile, back at the ranch" . . .God was leading me deeper and deeper into His presence until I hit a wall. I thought I was as deep as anyone could get, but that was just my foolishness. Life-changing events were coming together to catapult me into the power of Holy Spirit gifts.

My sister worked at the local hospital in Medical Records. Her job took her all over the building, and she was not comfortable with the spiritual atmosphere. So, she asked Chris, a Christian friend who was an experienced intercessor, to pray with her there. When she told me what was going on, I asked to join them. Years later, I am still praying with them, but I am in no way the same pray-er I was then.

We "walked" the hospital, discussing what we saw and felt and praying in the presence of God. Chris' way of praying was foreign to me, actually engaging with God to change atmospheres right in the moment! She taught me how to release burdens, to cast out darkness, to deliver others, to bring the goodness of God to earth... Our Tuesdays together became the highlight of my week. I never knew prayer could be so exciting!

We added Saturday and began walking the city. We would see changes almost immediately, and I was astounded again and again. Chris never forgot the prayer warriors who had plowed the ground before us, but I was lost in the excitement, blinded by pride. I couldn't wait to try out my "new abilities" in prayer.

I would go out on my own to fight against the darkness. (I urgently advise against this. I was arrogant and prideful, and it got me into trouble!) I walked right into New Age places, and I prayed this new way, determined to bring God into these "places of evil." I was going to save the world. Anyone (with wisdom) who tried to stop me just didn't know how powerful I was in the gifts of the Holy Spirit. *Sigh...*

I attended a school for a few years called "The School of the Supernatural." The goal was to activate and release the gifts of the Holy Spirit in healthy ways. One of the teachers had chosen me to accompany her on a prayer walk and I was eager to go. We went into the enemy camp and I, praying under her authority, witnessed a great battle. I saw in a vision a great army of angels facing a hoard of darkness. A trumpet sounded and they engaged. The fighting was fierce, and she and I were part of it, stationed on a hill as watchmen! God's angels prevailed, and His presence flooded the place.

A few weeks later, I revisited the place. I looked out from the vantage point where we had stood and savored the victory. "I had a hand in this. Look at the good work I did."

Then I saw it – the enemy creating another stronghold. I was livid. "Who were they to think they could do that?"

I jumped back into my car and sped off to park in the middle of the enemy camp. I had proved myself in battle. This would not stand!

Jumping out of my car, I looked around. There were demons all around me, but they were keeping their distance. It wasn't me; God had sent an angel to protect me, and they wanted nothing to do with <u>him</u>! The angel army was stationed above, and I called for them to come down and crush this force! I waved my arms and moved all around and they all just sat and stared at me; I must have been the afternoon's entertainment. I think back now and realize how foolish it all was. There I was, standing by my car waving my arms all around, calling out to invisible forces. It's God's mercy the men in white coats didn't come to haul me away!

We do not command angels; God does. God had not sent me there, I had. That there was an angel there to protect me is a testimony of God's love for me, not my "might in battle." *Sigh – again...*

After a while, I stopped, "God, why aren't these angels coming?"

Nothing. That was *so* the wrong prayer. Something inside of me (probably Holy Spirit trying to get my attention) knew that, and I began to worship. I just didn't know what else to do, and I couldn't turn tail and run (my pride again). I stood there and raised my arms to heaven praising and loving God and ignoring everything else around me. Suddenly, the angel army came storming down, and God's presence came bubbling up out of the ground. The enemy was trapped between the angels above and the golden presence below, and they were defeated.

I could take no credit for the victory. I had done nothing! This was a wake-up call, and I realized I had to learn from the beginning how to do this warfare thing.

Tim Sheets says, "The God-head is often described in scripture as releasing their ministry on the earth. . .through angels. So most certainly, if they release their ministries through angels, it should not be surprising that we, the heirs of God and joint-heirs with Christ, the sons and daughters of God, also need angels to partner with us to assist us in our ministries on the earth. . . God didn't make angels to see if He could do it! They are needed beings. Hebrews 1:14 says the heirs need angels to assist them in ministry. They are ministering spirits for the heirs."[1]

It is hard to believe, and you may think I'm nuts, but God sent an angel to me. He was big and strong, fierce and mighty in battle,

---

[1] Time Sheets, "Angel Armies" https://youtu.be/weB9iyKw5nQ

107

and he protected me for several years. I constantly learned by his example. He just seemed to be there whenever I was struggling. I watched him fight, and I learned to be brave. He never doubted the power of God with him, and I saw him time and again gain fearless victory in battle. When I struggled in prayer, I would feel alone, but when the breakthrough came, there he was celebrating the victory with me. He never spoke, but his actions connected to the Father were a wonder to behold and I was humbled in his presence. He was like a guardian angel for me.

I watched him fight and learned. But more importantly, I learned from his humility. When God's presence came, this fierce warrior would drop to his knees, honoring God with his whole being. I would watch God bless him and strengthen him. These intimate moments between Creator and created showed me the greatness of God more than any other. I knew the incredible strength of this warrior angel, his unshakable courage against overwhelming odds, the fierce, unbridled joy in his war cry, and I was allowed to see him submit himself humbly and wholly to God, honoring Him with himself. If this angel, who was so much more than I, did this, then I needed to learn the same.

When we submit to God, He begins to change our way of thinking to His. Old ways must go if we are to understand even a little of who God is and what He wants. If we do this, God will gently turn our hearts and minds to His, even if we don't understand that we're off track. The key is submission. Yielding to God, honoring God above all, will bring us to understanding.

There is a straightforward example of this in Isaiah 55. Isaiah has been interceding for Israel and Judah because they are miserable in exile. This man of God is under the gun. The people need hope, and they are pressuring him to give them a word they can hold on to. Isaiah is compassionate and feels their pain and oppression, yet God wants to deliver something different. So, God begins with a call to repentance:

"Hear Me, pursuers of righteousness, seekers of Jehovah; look to the rock from which you were cut, and to the hollow of the pit from which you were dug. Look to your father Abraham, and to Sarah who bore you. For he being but one I called him, and blessed him and increased him. (Isaiah 55:1-2)

"All you guys searching for meaning, you're looking in the wrong place. I made a nation out of one man (the rock from which you were cut). I created life where there was not life (the hollow of the pit from which you were dug). Remember this and know that I can save you."

Now Isaiah, seizing on a chance of escape from exile's misery, completely misses the message and bears witness to how great God is. It's true, it's just not the message.

"For Jehovah comforts Zion, He comforts all her desolations, and He makes her wilderness like Eden, and her desert like the garden of Jehovah; joy and gladness shall be found in it, thanksgiving and the voice of singing praise." (Isaiah 55:3)

This is wonderful praise, but if Isaiah is going to deliver the message God has for His people, he needs an attitude change. God said words of repentance, "Look to the rock and the pit from where you come from. Take an example from Abraham and Sarah. Look how I blessed his faith in me. Turn from your way and return to Me." This message of repentance seems to be lost in Isaiah's need to tell Israel some good news and affirming words.

God speaks again, confirming His dedication and explaining how His love will be made manifest (through Jesus Christ). This is mysterious stuff, prophetic words of deliverance that are difficult to grasp.

"Hear Me, My people; yea, give ear to Me, My nation. For a law shall go out from Me, and My justice I will make rest as light to peoples. My righteousness is near; My salvation went out; and My arms shall judge peoples; coasts shall wait on Me, and they shall hope on My arm. Lift up your eyes to the heavens, and look to the earth beneath; for the heavens vanish like smoke, and the earth shall wear out like a garment; and its inhabitants shall die in the same way, but My salvation shall be forever, and My righteousness shall not be broken. Hear Me, knowers of righteousness, the people of My law in their heart; do not fear the reproach of man, and do not be bowed from their blasphemings. For the moth shall eat them like a garment; yea, the moth worm shall eat them like wool. But My righteousness shall be forever, and My salvation generation to generation. (Isaiah 55: 4-8)

If we look to the grandeur of the heavens and the vast, untamed earth we live on, it all testifies to the greatness of the One who created it. We are awed by the sky and the earth, but it will all pass away. It's just dust in the wind compared to the eternity of God. And that "forever" is where we abide, that is the magnitude of His salvation. No man can touch it or harm our place in it. His salvation is eternal; from generation to generation.

Isaiah has not missed the words "do not fear the reproach of man" and is now repentant. He shifts his gaze from his own misery to God Himself and can't help but extol His virtues.

"Awake! Awake! Put on strength, arm of Jehovah. Awake, as in days of old, everlasting generations. . .Yes, the ransomed of Jehovah shall return and come to Zion with singing, and everlasting joy shall be on their head; gladness and joy shall overtake; sorrow and sighing shall flee." (Isaiah 55: 9-11)

Oh, how Isaiah wants God's redemptive power to save His people right now! But God knows the fullness of time has not yet arrived. God is talking about Jesus, and Isaiah is still lost in the present circumstances. Isaiah wants to deliver the message the people wants to hear, "God is coming to save us!" So, God has another go, slowly opening Isaiah's eyes to His reality.

"I, I am He comforting you. Who are you, that you should fear from man? He shall die! He is given as grass. And you forget your Maker Jehovah, who stretched out the heavens and founded the earth. And you dread continually, every day from the fury of the oppressor, since he was ready to destroy. . .But I am Jehovah your God, stirring up the sea and making its waves roar; Jehovah of hosts is His name. And I have put My words in Your mouth, and covered you in the shade of My hand, to plant the heavens and found the earth, and to say to Zion, You are My people." (Isaiah 55:12-16)

God says, "Isaiah, I'm sharing this with you because you need to know the joy that will come, but your heart is not right with Me. Just like everyone else you are afraid of what people will think. You're focused on earthly things instead of heavenly things. Remember how great I am and take comfort in that. I, the Creator God, have given you the words you are to say. Have confidence and say them all to the people."

Now Isaiah's attitude is fully changed. Instead of asking God to overwhelm the people into praise, he calls the people to repentance.

"Awake! Awake! Rise up, O Jerusalem, who drank the cup of His fury from the hand of Jehovah; you drank the bowl of the cup of reeling; you fully drained it. No guide is for her among all the sons she has borne; and none takes her by the hand of all the sons she made to grow. Those two things came to you; who shall wail for you?" (Isaiah 55:17-19a)

"Wake up, Jerusalem! You've been reeling under God's discipline too long. There is no one teaching wisdom and no sons taking care of you. Who is crying for you now? Wake up and see God!"

God knew the nation wanted words of comfort (Isaiah's first message) but needed words of discipline (Isaiah's second message). Hearts repented and opened to Him. Now they can hear God speak.

Isaiah could not hear the word of God through the cloud of his insecurity. He needed the approval of others and he let that color his message. God showed him a beautiful future for Jerusalem that moved Isaiah out of self-centeredness and into an overwhelming excitement about that future. Now he could clearly hear God's message and delivered some hard words to Israel. But even though those words were not the message they wanted, it was the very message they needed. They finally turned to God and He delivered them.

It is God's mercy ever-present that shapes us. Isaiah needed a heart change to deliver God's message of mercy. So, God moved Isaiah's heart and mind into His will so he could hear the message clearly. Only after Isaiah understood and obeyed did God do the same for His people (the intercessors go first!).

We must see past ourselves to clearly hear God's words. This was a hard lesson I was resisting. I was moving into spiritual depths I had never known, and God needed to do some more work before I could continue.

My whole life had been about people-pleasing. Be quiet so mom is happy. Do every musical thing possible to make dad happy. Be compliant to make my boyfriend happy. Behave and do your work to make the teacher happy. Act like a good girl to make God happy. Now I thought I was past that, but those old lies of life were still guiding me. "Be careful what you say. If someone is mad at you, that means you're a bad person." "Don't ever cry in front of people. They'll think you're weak." "Choose your friends wisely, or you won't get up in the world." I even taught Bible studies and preached sermons to show people how much I knew about God and scripture. I claimed their appreciation as my own, needing to satisfy my desire for their approval.

God now began to go after these man-pleasing, I-need-to-impress fears. Not just the easy ones, but even the anxieties I didn't know about that affected me without being aware. Then He went after the anger behind them even to the hurt that sprouted the anger. There were years of peeling away at this onion until only my pride remained.

Now, this was the root of it all. I had heavily invested in my pride. It was my protection against a hostile world. I could insulate myself against the attacks of others because "they didn't understand my pain" or "they really don't have the depth of knowledge that I have. How can I expect them to be mature?" I was the one who constantly corrected others because I was "helping" them. I didn't take risks because I didn't want to be seen to fail. When I taught or spoke in public, I was sure I was inspiring my audience. My little world was full of my success and brilliance. I'm really not exaggerating. I am ashamed to admit that I was a total snob.

Of course, I was so deeply immersed; I didn't see it. I really believed I was humble and had a servant's heart. The deception was so ingrained that when I was confronted with this pride, I was completely baffled why anyone would think that. Of course, I would think, "What did I say that they misinterpreted to come to that erroneous opinion?" Full of concern, I would move into conversation with the intent of clearing up the misunderstanding, which meant changing their mind. I must, again, apologize to anyone who has ever known me and ask for forgiveness.

When God began to show me just how awful this pride thing was, I was horrified. It colored everything, veiling truths and revelations God was trying to give me. It twisted everything into a box I could process. I began an intense campaign to rid myself of it once and for all. Trusted friends were given the responsibility of letting me know when I was being prideful. They were faithful to me and, though it was hard to hear, helped me to change behaviors.

My prayers began to be full of repentance. I wanted to love

God more than myself. That seemed the only way out. If I didn't care about me, then pride would have no importance, and I could let go. I gave Him all my fears, my doubts, my pain, my self-loathing, and my self-love. All the garbage and all the redeemable qualities were on the table.

He spoke to me in visions. I remember one where I was sitting at the bottom of a hill. It was dusky; grays and blacks. I looked up and saw Jesus standing at the top in all His brilliance, smiling at me and inviting me to join Him. But there was a rock wall between us, and I knew if I didn't tear it down, it would continue to keep us apart. I looked around for some tools, and there was nothing. I was desperate to get to Him, so I attacked the wall with my fingers, digging in between the stones to dislodge them and bring down that wall. He must have helped me because it came down, and I was able to run up to Him and hug Him. He held me in His arms, smiling and encouraging me. I felt like a little girl in the arms of her father. It was bliss.

He would take me back to that moment when I was in the throes of another hard battle. Remembering His arms around me, I would be encouraged to fight on knowing He waited on the other side. Remembering the humility of my warrior angel, I would submit to anything. Repentance, apologies, pleas for forgiveness, facing the onslaught of someone's anger knowing there is no answer and nothing I could say. Their ridicule was mine to bear because I had earned it with hard words and a stony heart, and yet He always lifted my burden and brought me to forgiveness.

"He was wounded for our transgressions; He was bruised for our iniquities; the chastisement of our peace was on Him; and with His wounds we ourselves are healed. All we like sheep have gone astray; we have each one turned to his own way; and Jehovah made meet in Him the iniquity of all of us. He was oppressed, and He was afflicted but He did not open His mouth. He was led as a lamb to the slaughter; and as a ewe before her shearers is dumb, so He opened not His mouth. . . He put His grave with the wicked; and with a rich man in His death; although He had done no violence, and deceit was not in His mouth. But Jehovah pleased to crush Him, to make Him sick, if He should put His soul as a guilt offering. (Isaiah 53:5-10, emphasis added)

Jesus had a choice. He could have chosen to forego the cross. This "if" is huge! What if Jesus had said, "No thanks, not doing that. It's too much." But He didn't. He loves us so much; He decided the cross was a price He could pay for us. How do you answer that kind of love if not with your whole heart and soul?

One day I was reliving a recent event that I had reacted to in pride and self-righteousness. I threw myself on my bed in tears. I thought I had gotten past all of this, but here it was again. I cried out to God to take it from me. How many times must I tear down a wall? I wanted *nothing* between us, but I couldn't seem to rid myself of this curse. "Rip it out, Lord. Even if I'm holding on, rip it out of my hands and get it out of me!" Sobbing and screaming in frustration, I felt helpless and fought despair.

Suddenly I couldn't move. My crying subsided as I lay motionless, only able to breathe. A deep coldness covered my body and sank into my bones. There was not a cell in my body that wasn't freezing. Curiously, I wasn't shivering or afraid. I knew it was God answering my prayer. I don't know how long I remained frozen in place, but eventually, it lifted. I still couldn't move, but now all was peace and calm. I felt light-headed and confused. I wasn't myself. My thoughts were different. My emotions were bare. I was confused and asked the Lord what had happened.

He began to show me my deliverance. The pride was finally gone, but I must be careful not to invite it back. Everything would be new, and I couldn't deal with life in any familiar way – any of that would open the door to pride again. Was I ready to face the world with no defenses? Was I ready to walk with no understanding of the world, learning as I went? Was I ready to trust God that much? This was a Gethsemane moment. I must choose to walk blindly with God. No defenses. No pearls of wisdom.

All I knew was I was free, and I wanted to stay free. For many months I was like a naïve child. Every encounter was new. Every fear was debilitating. No more could I hide behind the walls of pride. I must stand naked in the face of fear and trust God to protect me. Every joy was sheer happiness, no longer tainted by thoughts of unworthiness or distrust in its "fragile nature." I learned the unshakable strength and everlastingness of the joy that flows from the Kingdom of God.

Everything had God's hand on it. I went nowhere without praying and asking Him to come with me. I wanted nothing but Him, afraid of what my efforts would invite back into my life, and I would stay in bed rather than get up without Him there. My trusted friends helped me, protected me, and guided me back into maturity without prideful insecurity. I now pray with them knowing what they have done for me, how God used them to bring me to this freedom.

Visions and dreams are now frequent conversations. God knows I love puzzles, and He seems to never run out of experiences for me to figure out with Him. Prophetic words delivered are not as frequent as they once were. I believe that's because I no longer need to feel validated by someone's appreciation. God can use someone else, but mostly it's because I'm not forcing my need on His word. Silent prayers have taken the place of urgent conversations. Peace seems to be a gift He has increased in my soul and spirit.

"Guard the treasure you were given! Guard it with your life. Avoid the talk-show religion and the practiced confusion of the so-called experts. People caught up in a lot of talk can miss the whole point of faith." (1 Timothy 6:20-21, MSG)

It will be a life-long battle, but my victory is in Jesus. He bore the pain of my pride so He could help me overcome it. He is God, and I bow in humility before Him.

And the end result is...

As of the writing of this book, I have been single and unattached for 16 years. I never thought I could be happy living like this, but Jesus has never left me and continues to draw me ever deeper into His presence. It is God's radical changes that have given me contentment and joy in this new life.

"For My thoughts are not your thoughts; nor are your ways My ways, says Jehovah. For as the heavens are high from the earth, so My ways are high from your ways, and My thoughts from your thoughts. For as the rain and the snow goes down from the heavens and do not return there, but waters the earth and makes it bring forth and bud, and give seed to the sower and bread to the eater – so shall My word be, which goes out of My mouth; it shall prosper in what I sent it to do! For you shall go out with joy and be led out with peace. The mountains and the hills shall break out into song before you, and all the trees of the field shall clap the palm. Instead of the thorn-bush, the fir-tree shall come up; and it shall be for a name to Jehovah, for an everlasting sign that shall not be cut off." (Isaiah 55:8-13)

This is what He has for all of us if we yield to Him. Blessing, strength, joy, wholeness, the list is endless because He is infinite. He pours blessings and favor on the whole earth. When He speaks, every word He says accomplishes its purpose. Every word contains action and result, so every word is intentional and full of His presence.

Someone said to me once, "If it's too good to be true, it's probably God!" Let us walk into the truth that God is so much more than we can comprehend and accept freely everything He has for us. It is our trust in Him. It is His very nature for us.

DIGGING DEEPER

- **Read the following paraphrase of Isaiah 55:3.**

  "For Jehovah comforts me, He comforts all my desolations, and He makes my wilderness like Eden; and my desert like the garden of Jehovah; joy and gladness shall be found in it, thanksgiving and the voice of singing praise."

  Think about a deep hurt in your life and claim this promise for your own.

- **Read the following paraphrase of Isaiah 53: 5.**

  "For He was wounded for my transgressions. He was bruised for my iniquities; the chastisement of my peace was on Him; and with His wounds I am healed."

  Why would Jesus do such a thing for you?
  What does this tell you about your worth to God?

- **Read 1 Tim. 6: 20-21.** What treasure have you been given? How will you guard it? Why will you guard it?

PART 2

**The Community of Faith
Isaiah, Us and the Church**

How to build the house

"You also, as living stones, are being built up a spiritual house, a holy priesthood, to offer up spiritual sacrifices acceptable to God through Jesus Christ."
(1 Peter 2:5)

Our personal journey of faith is also the journey of the whole Church. The community of faith moves to maturity together just as we move toward it on our own. You can see every level of this journey in the Christian Church. Some congregations believe that the Bible is a rule book, a guide to living right. Others move from experience to experience; going to conferences or losing themselves in the ecstasy of worship every week. There are still more steeped in ministry, providing local needs, and supporting missionaries – loving the world through their programs. Revivals break out everywhere, calling for repentance and offering new levels of intimacy with God. I think the most powerful thing in the Church right now is the contemplative movement; finding God in the quietness of "soaking" in His presence, touching His heart and hearing His voice.

And we seem to fight for our vision of what the Church should be. Judging each other, we keep score and compare programs. How many souls were saved last year? How many people were helped? How many new members did we get? How many people came to our special programs? Which way is best? How do we know which Church is right?

The truth is - we need it all. The Church is glorious in its diversity, and there is no wrong or right in the corporate journey of faith. We, as individuals, need to express ourselves through all of it. So, too, does the Church. Yes, it's full of personal failures and flaws, but joining together as one to worship God is the most fantastic blessing that exists. This awesome God invites us to come not only individually, but *together* to be in His presence. He has reserved different revelations for the body of Christ, acting in unity (Ephesians 4:11-16). We need to know what that is supposed to look like and how to function in it.

The last chapters of Isaiah give us a pretty good look at the Church God wants. Part two of this book will examine these chapters, exposing God's heart for His Church and the world. But looking honestly at God's vision of the Church means we must acknowledge our failings. I'll share some of mine. Don't be afraid to recognize yours.

> "So says Jehovah: Keep justice and do righteousness, for My salvation is near to come, and My righteousness to be revealed. Blessed is the man who does this, and the son of man who lays hold on it, keeping sabbath, from defiling it, and keeping his hand from doing every evil." (Isaiah 56:1-2)

The Hebrew word used here for justice means the entire process of the law: the act, the place, the crime, the suit, and the penalty. We need to be aware of every aspect of our actions and the consequences of our words. If we walk in the power of God's word, the consequences will bless, not injure. Keeping justice means our lives are lived with an awareness of the future impact of our actions and words. Only God can lead us in justice, for only He knows the immediate and far-reaching future.

Righteousness means "to be or caused to be made right; to cleanse or clear yourself." We know we wear the righteousness of Christ (Ephesians 6:14), but there is action required of us to gain His garments; surrender, praise, worship, love, and prayer (Ephesians 4). If we are to "do righteousness," we must not only clothe ourselves in the presence of God but walk together as one in doing good.

"And [Jesus] Himself gave some to be apostles, some prophets, some evangelists, and some pastors and teachers, for the equipping of the saints for the work of ministry, for the edifying of the body of Christ, till we all come to the unity of the faith and of the knowledge of the Son of God, to a perfect man, to the measure of the stature of the fullness of Christ, . . .and speaking the truth in love, may grow up in all things into Him who is the head – Christ – from whom the whole body, joined and knit together by what every joint supplies, according to the effective working by which every part does its share, causes growth of the body for the edifying of itself in love." (Ephesians 4:11-16)

We are charged to grow into one perfect man, the likeness of Christ; so unified that receiving words from me is the same as receiving words from you, because we all speak the words of the Lord. We all do what the Savior tells us to. We are not robots, all tuned to the same frequency, but unified in our belief in Christ and honoring each other in love.

Blessed are the churches who understand this and lean into knowing God as a vital part of their corporate lives.

"Do not let the son of the foreigner speak, he who joins himself to Jehovah, saying, "Jehovah surely separates me from His people," and do not let the eunuch say, "Behold, I am a dried tree." For so says Jehovah to the eunuchs who keep My sabbaths and choose things I am pleased with, and take hold of My covenant: "I even will give to them in My house and in My walls a hand and a name better than sons and than daughters; I will give them an everlasting name, which shall not be cut off. And the sons of the alien who join themselves on Jehovah to serve Him, and to love Jehovah's name, . . .them I will bring to My holy mount and make them joyful in My house of prayer. Their burnt offerings and their sacrifices shall be accepted on

My altar, for My house shall be called a house of prayer for all peoples." (Isaiah 56:3-7)

"A new commandment I give to you, that you love one another, as I have loved you, that you also love one another. By this all will know that you are My disciples, if you have love for one another." (John 13:34-35)

We must honor and respect anyone who comes to God. Everyone who claims Jesus as Lord is deserving of our open doors and acceptance. God has chosen them; it is not for us to cause them to feel alienated or "less than." Even those who seem to have no value to the Church at all, God will give a place of honor in His house; a place that will last forever. If we are to walk in His will, we must acknowledge with humility **all** God's children.

I went back to college in my 40's to get a Master of Music degree. Joining a touring choir was required, and I became a member of a mixed choir full of 60 young voices. It was wonderful. I hadn't sung like that in years. So, we went on tour and were practicing in a church for a performance that evening. A homeless man wandered in and began to talk to himself in the back. It was very distracting, and we all got more and more upset with him. Really, we were all just standing there miffed because he had interrupted our rehearsal.

Suddenly, a young man standing on the edge of a riser left us and quietly walked down the aisle to where this man was sitting. He sat down with him and began to talk. They had a quiet conversation while we continued our singing. Eventually, this young man helped the older man to the door and returned to the choir.

Now, we were not members of that Church, but the homeless man did not know that. I spoke to that young man later and learned that this homeless man was looking for help. That teenager was more compassionate than the 59 of us. He was the only one truly "churchlike" at that moment. That homeless man entered the Church to find something of God there, maybe our music brought him in, and a teenager was the only one who responded to his need in love and concern. We who stayed on the risers and sang, ignoring the homeless man's plight, were "rewarded" by the appreciation of our director. That young man was reprimanded in front of all of us, publicly humiliated for leaving the rehearsal, but he was tuned to God's heart and was the only one in the room truly doing the right thing.

God's decree is "My house shall be called a house of prayer for *all* the people." He has decreed. If we are to keep justice and do righteousness, we must act on that decree.

"All the peoples" - His holiness looks messy to us. Popular, homeless, mentally ill, influential, criminals, addicts, prim and proper, poor, rich – these are all *our* perceptions. God sees our hearts and calls every one of His children to Himself. He doesn't care what circumstance the world has brought to anyone. How can we then prefer our judgment over His? The Church is not to choose, but to shepherd *all* whom God brings.

"Unless the Lord builds the house, they labor in vain who build it" (Psalm 127:1), God will build, or we will fail. And when God builds, we need to bend into His construction.

> "His watchmen are blind, they all do not know, they are all dumb dogs. . . yea, dogs greedy of soul; they do not know satisfaction. And they are shepherds, they know not discernment: they all look to their own way, each one to their own way, each one for his own gain, from his own end, saying, 'Come, and let me bring wine, and let us gulp down fermented drink; and tomorrow shall be as this day, great, exceedingly abundant.'" (Isaiah 56:9-12)

And here we are building our own house. In our own wisdom, we are blind. We are greedy for the fulfillment of our dreams and compromise ourselves to attain it. We don't realize what we're doing, but while we think we are shepherding the flock, we are motivated by our own needs and self-centered in our ministry.

We might as well be throwing a drunken party to enjoy all our gains.

We can't tell what is good or bad, who belongs and who doesn't. When we build from our own understanding, we make a house that will crumble under the least bit of pressure. There is no everlasting blessing in something created by limited minds who cannot see into or understand eternity. We take our abundance for granted and do not adequately prepare for the future because we have no discernment; we *do not know*.

Only God knows how to move His kingdom into this world. Only God can see the big picture. We can create a church that we're comfortable in, but is it really about us?

Daily the Church faces this crossroad. Are we to trust God and allow Him to build the house however that looks, or are we going to follow what we like and build the house from our own experience and understanding? Our house is easier to build, but all the blessing and joy is in God's house.

DIGGING DEEPER

- **Read Isaiah 56: 1-2.** Why is it important for the church to keep the sabbath? List 4 additional reasons that aren't revealed in this scripture.

- **Read Isaiah 56: 3-7.** Who are the "sons of the foreigner" and the "eunuchs" in your church? In your neighborhood? What can your church do to cause them to rejoice and feel like family?

- **Read Psalm 127:1.** How is God building your church? The world-wide church?

We must face our wrongdoing
Before the church can rise

"I see right through your work. You have a reputation for vigor and zest, but you're dead, stone-dead. Up on your feet! Take a deep breath! Maybe there's life in you yet. But I wouldn't know it by looking at your busywork, nothing of God's work has been completed. Your condition is desperate. Think of the gift you once had in your hands, the Message you heard with your ears – grasp it again and turn back to God." (Revelation 3:1b-3, MSG)

When the declaration of independence was signed in 1776, it defined America to the world and started a revolution. Our founding fathers had a conviction that led them on a journey down a road of no return. The fighting was fierce and, more than once, George Washington thought that all might be lost. But, through prayer and sheer grit, the revolution was won. The result, a country never seen before, born out of an "Appeal to Heaven;" no monarch, no formal aristocracy, all men (and eventually all people) acknowledged as having value and rights beyond economic or social class. This fragile country built on the ideals of a few men rose to become the most powerful country in the world.

The Church needs to return to the conviction of *our* founding fathers. We need to stand on God's promises, set our face in determination, and make a declaration of holiness that will start a Godly revolution and redefine the Church to the world. Our God is the Creator of everything and everyone. The Church, <u>His</u> Church, should rise to be the most powerful blessing in the world.

A declaration for the Church (Isaiah 57 paraphrased)

We confess that we are insensitive to the suffering of Your children around the world. It doesn't occur to us that our actions might be making other lives miserable. We say, "They go to heaven, their misery is over." We are so lost in our own thoughts that we don't even know what we've done. Forgive our callousness.

We confess that we judge wrongly those who are different from us. We have rebelled against You and Your call to love everyone, even those we don't want to love. Forgive our selfishness.

We confess that although many of us go through the motions of religion, most of us don't even try anymore. We, all of us, have created gods of work, love, sex, money, possessions, you name it. We walk away from truth and trade it for the morality of the moment – whatever seems right must be OK. We sacrifice our children on the altar of political correctness. Deciding we know what's best for us, we have made plenty of room in our lives for our own desires and ambitions, following them down even to hell. We dress up our ideas in a beautiful array and costly perfumes and call them sacred and holy. When You bring us to face what we've done, our lives will go up in smoke-totally meaningless and wrong.

But You say that anyone who runs to You for help You will help. You will bless them and give them Your holy land. So, we run to You, Lord, to save us. Save Your Bride. Stir us up to build a road of righteousness, free of obstruction, where everyone seeking You can travel safely. You live in the high and holy places, but You also live with depressed and broken people. You put a new spirit in us and lift us up on our feet again. Remember Your people, Lord. Remember Your Church. Though we have forgotten our roots, do not be angry at our shame and rebellion, but heal us, lead us, and comfort us. Create in us a new language of praise. Deliver Your peace to Your Church and Your people. Create in us a clean heart, O God.

Are we ready to risk everything for a future we can only dream of? Is a vital, energetic church full of the power of the Holy Spirit worth paying everything for?

The early Church was extraordinary. Our founding fathers showed us that we can surely fulfill Jesus' words, "Most assuredly, I say to you, he who believes in Me, the works that I do he will do also, and greater works than these he will do, because I go to My Father." (John 14:12)

Jesus didn't say, "I'm only talking to the Apostles." Nor did He say, "This is for the next 100 years and then you won't need it anymore." He said, "He who believes in Me." That's you and me, that's everyone in the Church who claims Him as Lord.

Why are our shadows not healing people like Peter's? (Acts 5:14-16) Why are we not accepting the presence of angels as a fact of life like the early believers? (Acts 12:13-15) Why are we not praying together until God shows Himself in power like the disciples in the upper room? (Acts 2) Why are we willing to live lesser lives when God desires to pour Himself on us? (Isaiah 44:3)

We have forgotten our roots. Lord, create in us a new language of praise. Deliver Your Church from our complacency and create in us a clean heart, O God.

 DIGGING DEEPER

- List 3 ways the church been insensitive to the suffering of God's children. Take a few moments to pray/repent for the church.

- List 3 ways the church has wrongly judged others. Take a few moments to pray/repent for the church.

- List 5 "idols" in the church and pray for God to take them down.

- What do you think the "road of righteousness" looks like for your church? How would you like to see your church move into deeper relationship with God? Pray for that right now.

When we mess up. . .

> "For He who is mighty has done great things for me, and holy is His name. And His mercy is on those who fear Him from generation to generation." (Luke 1:49-50)

Our prayers of repentance will not go unheard. God is faithful to correct us, taking us through the difficulty and pain of repentance and back into a life and community of caring.

> "Call out with the throat! Do not spare. Lift up your voice like the trumpet! And show My people their rebellion and their sins to the house of Jacob. Yet they seek Me day by day and desire knowledge of My ways. As a nation that has done right, and not forsaking the judgment of their God, they ask Me about judgments of righteousness; they desire to draw near to God. They say, 'Why have we fasted, and You did not see? We have afflicted our soul, and You did not acknowledge.' Behold, on the day of your fast you find pleasure and you drive all your laborers hard." (Isaiah 58:1-3)

These Jews were doing everything right. They were following the fasts and festivals, running through all the rituals in the temple; doing everything required of them. But their motivation was all wrong. Instead of loving and serving God, they were trading with Him, "We do this and now You do that." They were acting like they were equal with God and entitled to lord it over others.

God uses their fasts as an example. A fast was to seek God and humble yourself, making yourself weak and more dependent on

God; to deny yourself and seek the Lord in earnest. But they used their fast to feel superior – working their employees and slaves extra hard and indulging their egos in their "holiness." God can't honor that.

> "Look! You fast for strife, and for debate, and to strike with the fist of wickedness. Do not fast as today, to sound your voice in the high place. Is this like the fast I will choose, a day for a man to afflict his soul? To bow his head down like a bulrush, and he spreads sackcloth and ashes? Will you call to this as a fast, and a day of delight to Jehovah? Is this not the fast I have chosen; to open hands of wickedness, to undo thongs of the yoke, and to let the oppressed ones go free; even that you pull off every yoke? Is it not to break your bread to the hungry, that you should bring the wandering poor home? When will you see the naked and cover him; and you will not hide yourself from your flesh?" (Isaiah 58:4-7)

Israel's fasting made them feel self-righteous. They argued and debated their points and opinions with each other until it came to blows of shame and accusation. The pride they felt about their "purity of thought" made them stubborn, polarizing the nation and the Church over doctrine and theology.

Are we not the same? How many churches arose because of stubborn arguments over theology? Oh, I can hear you breathe in to start a debate with me right now about the truth of your beliefs.

At the risk of sounding blasphemous, let me say that God is not concerned with *our* belief systems. The rituals and behaviors we associate with holiness are not a priority with God, but a construct of man. They are good if they lead us to God. But so much of the time they are the routine we're comfortable in, creating the same encounter every week. There is no growth, no deeper connection, no friendship there.

God turned their idea of fasting upside-down. Instead of making themselves more holy, they were to spend their lives leading others to holiness. Here is what God is saying. "You want to know Me? Then open your heart and your home to the homeless, have mercy on your workers, free the slaves – even to the point of allowing them lives of leisure like yours. Give away the bounty I have given you to care for the poor, the homeless, and the naked – even to the point of your own nakedness. That is how much you are called to love and care for your fellow man."

"Then your light shall break as the dawn, and your healing shall spring up quickly; and your righteousness shall go before you, the glory of Jehovah shall gather you. Then you shall call, and Jehovah will answer; you shall cry; and He shall say, 'Here I am.' If you put the yoke away from among you, the pointing of the finger, and the speaking of vanity; and if you let out your soul to the hungry, and satisfy the afflicted soul, then your light shall rise in the darkness, and your gloom shall be as the noonday. And Jehovah shall always guide you, and satisfy your soul in dry places, and support your bones. And you shall be like a watered garden, and like a spring of water whose waters do not fail. And those who come of you shall build the old ruins; you shall rear the foundations of many generations; and you shall be called, the repairer of the breach, the restorer of paths to live in." (Isaiah 58:8-12)

Look what happens when we give ourselves to others! Suddenly our lives will change; healing will come quickly, righteousness will clear our paths, and we will be bathed in the glory of God! God will answer our prayers. All oppression and depression will be as nothing, because God will always lead us, satisfy us, and support us.

His presence in us will nurture future generations. His goodness rebuilds lives and creates bridges of love and understanding that last forever. The world will see this and recognize the power of the love of God to repair the breaches between people. They will clearly see the goodness of following Jesus and come to the Church for deliverance and blessing.

This is God's grace. In His upside-down kingdom, only those who truly humble themselves before Him will be exalted up to places of honor. Everything we are searching for, everything we want for our Church: recognition, wisdom, righteousness, honor, etc. comes from a servant's heart.

"Then [Jesus] came to Capernaum. And when He was in the house He asked them, 'What was it you disputed among yourselves on the road?' But they kept silent, for on the road they had disputed among themselves who would be the greatest. And He sat down, called the twelve, and said to them, 'If anyone desires to be first, he shall be last of all and servant of all.'"
(Mark 9:33-35)

Heidi Baker is a good example of this teaching. She has a Ph.D. from Oxford, runs a multi-million-dollar ministry that reaches across the globe, and is a sought-after speaker at conferences everywhere. No less than 10,000 churches are included in her ministry. Yet, her greatest joy is serving "the one in front of her." She will sit in the dirt and pull worms from a sick man's foot. She will spend the day at the garbage dump, slogging through the rot and decay of people's waste to talk to a child who needs to be loved. The love of Jesus compels her to act. The power of the Holy Spirit sustains her with joy.

She is willing to be last. In fact, I don't think she even cares where she is in line! The point is to forget about yourself. Last, first, what does it matter? It's not about us. It's about Him.

"If you turn your foot away because of the sabbath, from doing what you please on My holy day, and call the sabbath a delight, glorified to the holiness of Jehovah; and shall glorify it, away from doing your own ways, from finding your own pleasure of speaking your word; then you shall delight yourself in Jehovah. And I will cause you to ride on the heights of the earth, and make you eat with the inheritance of your father, Jacob. For the mouth of Jehovah has spoken." (Isaiah 58:13-14)

"If you love Me more than yourself" . . . Everything we want or need is here in this thought. His unlimited resources He freely gives to those He can trust with such riches.

And the world is watching. I once heard someone say, "Christians read the Bible, but the world reads the Christians." Our lives are a testimony for or against Christ; there is no middle ground. If we live lives of self-indulgence; going to Church when we feel like it, speaking our mind just because we had a thought, indulging in pleasure, taking offense instead of offering forgiveness, then the world sees a God who is shallow and meaningless.

But if we honor God with our time, thoughts, and actions, then He will bless us with His joy and strength. If we love Him with all the love He gives us; we will move into mental and physical health. He will provide for us, even giving us favor in the eyes of the world, and the world will see a living God who is relevant and victorious. The Church must live like this, so the world will "read" the truth about God.

"Seek first the kingdom of God and His righteousness and all these things will be added to you. (Luke 12:31)

What things? The light of understanding, healing of body and soul, a church held in the glory of God, an answer to every prayer, reliable provision for our lives. The wisdom that will be known through many generations, because our children will continue the work God gives us to do. The world will acknowledge our contributions and call us peacemakers and builders of goodness. God will be our everlasting joy and give us an eternal inheritance.

Some will say, "That's too good to be true." "That's pie-in-the-sky faith." But I say I will stand on the promises of God because:

"[Jesus] has always been and always will be for us a resounding 'YES!' For all of God's promises find their 'yes' of fulfillment in Him. And as His 'Yes' and our 'Amen' ascend to God, we bring Him glory!"
(2 Corinthians 1:19-20, TPT)

DIGGING DEEPER

- **Read Isaiah 58: 8-12**. The glory of the Lord revealed through us! What must the church do to make that happen? What can you do? Pray for that to happen right now.

- **Read Isaiah 58: 13-14**. What are the blessings that come to us when we keep the sabbath? Why do you think the sabbath is so important to God?

- *If we honor God with our time, thoughts and actions, then He will bless us with His joy and strength.* Explain what this statement tells you about the nature of God. How or why does that cause the church to rejoice?

We can change the world!

"For we do not wrestle against flesh and blood, but against principalities, against powers, against the ruler of the darkness of this age, against spiritual hosts of wickedness in the heavenly places." (Ephesians 6:12)

What hope there is in God! What a life we can have! What a church we can be! He has given us everything!!!

"Arise, shine; for your light has come, and the glory of Jehovah has risen on you! For behold, the darkness shall cover the earth, and gross darkness the peoples. But Jehovah shall rise on you, and His glory shall be seen on you. (Isaiah 60:1-2)

There are two kinds of darkness, darkness and gross darkness. The darkness that covers the earth is the spiritual powers of evil who exist. The gross darkness is the additional works of deception and bondage those powers exert over the people on the earth.

"The thief does not come except to steal, and to kill, and to destroy. I have come that they may have life, and that they may have it more abundantly." (John 10:10)

This is Jesus interpreting Isaiah for us. Satan and his forces (the darkness) come to steal, kill, and destroy (the actions of gross darkness), but Jesus brings life and light. So much so that we shine in His presence! That light has the power to make darkness (and gross darkness) flee.

Therefore submit to God. Resist the devil and he will flee from you." (James 4:7)

I had a friend who, at the end of her life, was tormented by hallucinations and mysterious pains. Her fear of her fragility just made everything worse. Finally, she was confined to a wheelchair, barely able to walk. She moved to an assisted living facility because she could no longer care for herself. We had been good friends for many years, so I was a frequent visitor at the home where she lived.

One day we were talking about Jesus and she asked me to pray for her. I sat with her and began to seek the Lord on her behalf. I don't remember everything I prayed, but when I started to declare that the light of God increase in her, there was a dramatic change in her demeanor. She looked at me with venom in her eyes. Her eyes dilated to full black, and she stared at me like she wanted me dead. Her head was moving like a charmed snake. This was a woman I had never seen before.

I was not going to stop. This evil had revealed itself and now it was time for it to go. I moved behind her and laid my hands on her head, continuing to pray for Jesus to increase His presence in her. Every muscle in her body seemed to tense up and resist. Eventually, she relaxed, and I felt released. She was slumped in her chair, limp and unresponsive. After about 5 minutes she recovered and seemed normal, but the episode had been so dramatic that she was immediately taken to the emergency room. A doctor's exam showed nothing wrong. She had no markers for stroke, heart attack, seizure, or any other physical ailment.

She had been delivered. Without the influence of evil, she felt peace and lightness for the first time in many years. Suddenly, people and circumstances that had been working against her began to shift dramatically. She was happy for the first time in ages. Her daughter found a new doctor who changed her meds, and soon her hallucinations stopped. Her physical therapist saw a change in her strength and gave her a new regimen of exercises that enabled her to transfer in and out of cars and walk a little, which gave her a lot more freedom. She always read her Bible, but now she was finding new revelations and joy in scriptures she had known her whole life. In every way, her life got better. God's light and presence brought her new freedom, joy, and strength.

We all have this light, this power to make evil flee. It is God, nothing to do with us. When we release it, things change. "He who is in you is greater than he who is in the world." (1 John 4:4) As individuals, we can be the vessels of deliverance for our piece of the world. But when we worship together as a church and move in unity, that light is multiplied until the world cannot deny it.

"And nations shall walk to your light, and kings to the brilliance of your dawning. Lift up your eyes all around and see; they are all assembling; they are coming to you. . .For the abundance of the sea shall be turned to you; the force of nations shall come to you. . .they shall come up for acceptance on My altar; I will glorify the house of My glory." (Isaiah 60:3-7)

When God's glory shines brightly on His people, the world cannot ignore it. Hundreds of thousands of people shall respond (nations), and governments and leaders (kings) will turn to the Lord because of our shining, but we can't let that go to our head, nor can we make that our ultimate goal. Let *Him* do that. We are the light, the beacon that shines on Jesus for everyone who comes.

"And the sons of the stranger shall build your walls, and their kings shall serve you. For I struck you in My wrath, but I pitied you in My favor. So your gates shall be always open; they shall not be shut day or night, so that men may bring to you the force of nations, and that their kings may be led. For the nations and the kingdom that will not serve you shall perish; yea, the nations shall be utterly destroyed." (Isaiah 60:10-12)

All things come from God. This is never made more evident than right here in Isaiah. "I struck you in My wrath, but I pitied you in My favor." God's favor brings peace – so much that the city gates will never have to be shut to protect the citizens. Trade and access will happen 24 hours a day. No one will attack or lay siege to the city. Anyone who does not serve the servants of God will be destroyed before they can gather an army! Abundant prosperity comes from His favor.

The church must adopt this way of being. Accepting the peace of God (which we all want and pray for) is never closing the doors to anyone. We forget the second part of "Unless God builds the house, they who build it labor in vain." Psalm 127:1 goes on to say, "Unless God guard the house, the watchman stays awake in vain." It is God who will guard the house He is building. We must trust Him to guard and protect so we are free to serve the servants of God. He will give us the wisdom to know how He wants us to help Him. Sometimes it's very surprising!

One Saturday, I joined a missionary group from out of town that was leading a training session on street ministry. We spent some time learning how to coordinate our approach, and one word of advice was to assign someone to be "lookout" and talk to the people who were curious about what we were doing while we were ministering to someone else. This person wasn't to push them away, just engage them so they didn't interrupt any prayers that might be happening.

Then we went to a tourist district in my town. This street has been thoroughly gentrified; wine tasting rooms, specialty restaurants, gift shops, etc. There is special parking for tourist buses. It is a very busy place, and we were there mid-morning on a Saturday – lots of people everywhere.

As the day progressed, our group met two wonderful ladies from out of town and began to talk to them. It was a pleasant conversation, comfortable and light, full of wonderful testimonies. Suddenly, I realized there was no lookout. I decided instead of interrupting the conversation to point this out so the leader could assign one, I would just do it. But Jesus very clearly told me to get back in the conversation. I thought, "But who is going to protect Your ministry?" and He said, "Leave that to Me."

OK. I didn't know what to think, but I rejoined the conversation. Words of knowledge and prophecy were flowing for these ladies, and I got lost in this move of God. Suddenly, Jesus said, "OK. Now you be the lookout." So, I took a step outside the group to look around. There was no-one on the street: no moving cars, no people in doorways, NOTHING! I was shocked. Even when the shops are closed there are always a few people milling about, looking in windows. At this moment our little group were the only people on the whole street!

God is perfectly capable of protecting His house. We must trust Him to do it so we can get on with the work He's given us to do.

"The glory of Lebanon shall come to you; the juniper, the box-tree, and the cypress together, to beautify the place of My sanctuary; yea, I will glorify the place of My feet. Also the sons of your afflicters shall come bowing to you. And all who despised you shall fall at the soles of your feet. And they shall call you The City of Jehovah, the Zion of the Holy One of Israel. Instead of your being forsaken and hated, so that no one passes through, I will make you for everlasting majesty, a joy of many generations. You shall also suck the milk of nations, and you shall suck the breast of kings. And you shall know that I, Jehovah, am your Savior and your Redeemer, the mighty One of Jacob." (Isaiah 60: 13-16)

Here again, we must never forget that God's prosperity – although we benefit from it – is for His glory. What happens to us reflects our relationship with God, and it is a corporate responsibility. We give Him the glory and the gifts, and He uses them to "beautify the place of My sanctuary; yea, I will glorify the place of My feet." We are the place of His sanctuary, so His light shines through us. The church is where He places His feet, so His blessing flows to her. Where He stands is glorified, and because He is reflected in us, those who once hated us will fall at our feet, and God will be glorified again through us.

Now God gives us some "insteads." Instead of no one wanting to associate with us or even do business with us, He will raise us so high in public opinion that our reputation and wisdom will bless many generations. Instead of working hard for resources, the basic resources of other countries will be made available to us; even leaders will open their most treasured resources for us to use.

God is the only One who can so completely change our circumstances; there is no way we could begin to do this ourselves. My crazy life is a testimony to that! The transformation will be so complete that we will know without a doubt that God has done this and that He is our Savior.

This will not happen for a church who desires all these things. God does this to glorify Himself, not us. The church must be "the bride." Our eyes, our heart, our desire must be only for Him. Only then are we ready to be blessed like this.

If the blessings come while we are looking for them (for whatever reason), they will destroy us, feeding those insecurities and desires that are self-serving. If we want and desire the gifts and miracles and blessings instead of the source, then the very things we are praying for will be our downfall. The accolades of the world will feed our egos, and we will not give God credit for it all. Oh, we may say the words, but remember that God knows the heart. He doesn't care about actions or confessions unless our love for Him drives them.

God's plan for His church is to be an everlasting testimony of His love for the world. It is not love to burden someone with responsibilities they are not ready to bear. That is not the way the Bridegroom loves His bride. And the bride needs to trust the Bridegroom.

Keep your eyes on His beauty and your heart tuned to His love, and the blessings will flow. And we will know who is providing such a life and we will praise Him for His salvation. He will shine so brightly in our lives that the sun and the moon will seem dull and lifeless. Our sun and moon will be God. Our beauty will be

God. And God will be with us forever.

We read this and say, "That's great, but not in my lifetime." "The world's a mess. I can't see that happening." or "This is heaven, right? Can't possibly happen on earth until Jesus comes back."

"So Jesus said to them again, 'Peace to you! As the Father has sent Me, I also send you.' And when He had said this, He breathed on them, and said to them, 'Receive the Holy Spirit.'" (John 20:21-22)

The Father sent Jesus with the Holy Spirit (descending on Him like a dove at His baptism). The Holy Spirit remained in and on Jesus for the duration of His ministry. So, when Jesus says, "As the Father has sent Me, I also send you" He's saying that everything He has we also have and everything He did we are to do. This includes the Holy Spirit abiding in and with us, empowering us to act with authority.

"For the kingdom of God is not eating and drinking, but righteousness and peace and joy in the Holy Spirit." (Romans 14:17)

The kingdom of God is not like earthly things but exists fully in the Holy Spirit and manifests in righteousness, peace, and joy. When the Holy Spirit descended on Jesus and remained, that meant Jesus had the kingdom of God complete in Himself for His ministry. He sends us out the exact same way. So, *we have the kingdom of God complete in ourselves through the Holy Spirit.*

With this incredible Spirit waiting in us to bring God's kingdom to earth, why are we not praying, "Holy Spirit release Yourself" every day!? He wills that His people, His church, be empowered in the world. That means it is within our power to change the environment around us to reflect the light of God!

I learned this a few years ago. I had just left a meeting where something had happened that triggered feelings of total inadequacy and fear. Feelings of despair were drowning me, and I was collapsing into tears. I drove to a quiet place and parked, entertaining emotions of self-doubt and condemnation.

My prayer was, "Why, Lord? Why is this happening to me?"

I was moving into helplessness and self-pity, the heart of the enemy's camp.

God reminded me that was the wrong prayer. Graham Cooke teaches that in such moments, the questions should be, "What does this mean and What must I do?"

So, I made a U-turn, asked the right questions, and God gave me a vision.

I saw myself in a very black place, no light at all. I knew the blackness was all the negative emotions I was feeling, but there was a small ball of light inside of me, just waiting there.

Suddenly, Jesus said, "You light up the place."

What? I had no idea how to do that. The light did not respond to my commands, nor did it communicate in any way. I tried everything I could think of, but that little ball of light just stayed there, glowing quietly inside of me.

I finally realized it was Holy Spirit, and now I understood that light was in no way going to submit to me. I threw up my arms and praised the Lord and invited Holy Spirit to release Himself. Suddenly, the whole place was awash in golden light, and there was life everywhere! The light radiated from my body and, if I yielded to it, it shone as bright as the sun. In the darkness of self-absorption (my problems, my fears, my feelings), I was completely blind to the life of God around me. But when Holy Spirit released God's light everything was clear, and everything was beautiful. All my feelings disappeared in the joy of the Lord!

"The sun shall not still be your light by day, or the brightness of the moon give you light; but Jehovah shall be for everlasting light to you, and your God for your beauty. Your sun shall not set any more; and your moon shall not withdraw; for Jehovah will become your everlasting light; and the days of your mourning shall end.

And your people shall all be righteous; they shall possess the earth forever, a branch of My planting, a work of My hands, to beautify Myself." (Isaiah 60:19-21)

Do we deny the power of God at our fingertips because it is too much to consider seriously? Lift your eyes and see. Go to God with your questions, your doubts, your overwhelmed mind and let Him calm your fear with faith, enlarge your heart to rejoice, and reflect His light to the world today! His blessings are ours NOW! His kingdom is ours NOW! Jesus has given us everything, and the Holy Spirit burns to glorify our Savior through us!

"Most assuredly, I say to you, he who believes in Me, the works that I do he will do also, and greater works than these he will do, because I go to My Father. And whatever you ask in My name, that I will do, that the Father may be glorified in the Son." (John 14:12-13)

These words Jesus told His disciples were seared into their hearts and were part of the foundation of the new church. Are we bold enough to follow and claim this promise for ourselves?

DIGGING DEEPER

- **Read Isaiah 60: 1-2.** How does Jehovah "rise on you?" On the church? What does that look like to the world?

- **Read Isaiah 60: 3-7.** "Lift up your eyes all around and see . . ." What is God calling you to see? What does that look like in your church today? In the world-wide church?

- **Read Isaiah 60: 19-21.** Why do you think God wants to "beautify" Himself? Is the world attracted to beauty? What does that mean for the church?

- Think of 3 ways the church displays beauty. Take a few moments to thank God for blessing the church.

We are trees of righteousness

When Jesus began His ministry, He stood in the synagogue to read the scripture, found Isaiah 61, and read this:

"The Spirit of the Lord is upon Me, because He has anointed Me to preach the gospel to the poor; He has sent Me to heal the brokenhearted, to proclaim liberty to the captives and recovery of sight to the blind, to set at liberty those who are oppressed; to proclaim the acceptable year of the Lord." (Luke 4: 18-19)

Then He closed the book and sat down. Everyone was looking at Him, and He said, "Today this scripture is fulfilled in your hearing."

In Jesus' day reciting the first verse or two of a portion of the scripture referred the listener to the entirety of that passage. So, Jesus is not just saying He is the fulfillment of the first few verses, but the entire chapter. Every precious word Isaiah wrote hundreds of years before is now alive and sitting in the synagogue!

"The Spirit of the Lord Jehovah is on Me, because Jehovah has anointed Me to preach the gospel to the meek. He has sent Me to bind up the broken hearted, to proclaim liberty to captives, and complete opening to the bound ones: to proclaim the acceptable year of Jehovah, and the day of vengeance of our God; to comfort all who mourn; to appoint to those who mourn in Zion, to give them beauty instead of ashes, the oil of joy instead of mourning, the mantle of praise instead of the spirit of infirmity; so that one calls them trees of righteousness,

151

the planting of Jehovah, in order to beautify Himself."
(Isaiah 61: 1-3)

Story after story in the gospels demonstrates the love of Jesus through His ministry of healing and miracles. After being brought to tears by the sadness and fears of the widow of Nain, he raised her son from the dead and gave him back to her; oil of joy instead of mourning (Luke 7:11-15). Repeatedly He "healed all who were brought to Him" or "He healed all the sick" or He fed all the weary people; giving them the mantle of praise in exchange for their suffering. He wept at Lazarus' tomb, not because Lazarus was dead, but because of the overwhelming sadness of people Jesus loved. Then He raised Lazarus and gave him back to his sisters; changing their ashes of sorrow into the beauty of love and literally unbinding Lazarus from the dead (John11:38-44). Jesus was continuously fulfilling these words of Isaiah.

John says, "And there are also many other things that Jesus did, which if they were written one by one, I suppose that even the world itself could not contain the books that would be written." (John 21:25)

After Jesus has healed the wounds of the people and turned their troubles into joy and praise, He says, "so that one calls them trees of righteousness, the planting of Jehovah, in order to beautify Himself."

We are those trees of righteousness. We who believe and have accepted Jesus into our heart have been "planted" by His streams of living water, constantly nourished by His presence and Holy Spirit. We are healed, restored, given all the wonderful gifts Isaiah listed, and as we grow in this relationship, the world sees more and more of God in us. We are beautiful in His peace and joy, which glorifies God to the world.

And these trees are planted together by His streams of living water. It is all of us together in the "forest" of the church who will do these things. God does not say, "You are a tree.' He says, "They are trees." "They" is us, the church, the community of God's people who move with Him in the earth.

"And they shall build old ruins, they shall raise up former desolations; and they shall restore the waste cities, ruins of generations and generations. (Isaiah 61:4-5)

Everything that has been laid waste we shall restore. Jesus repaired the ruins of many lives, and now we are charged to do the same. The emotional ruins of a life. The physical ruins of a neighborhood. The spiritual ruins of misinterpreted scripture or bad teaching. It's all in need of resurrection and healing. Through Jesus we have the power to do it. We, the church through the power of the Holy Spirit, are the "they," the trees of righteousness that bear good fruit for the world. Generations of suffering and disrepair will change in the light of His love shining through us.

"But you shall be called, Priests of Jehovah; it will be said of you, Ministers of God. You shall eat the riches of nations, and you shall revel in their glory." (Isaiah 61:6)

In Jesus' day, only male descendants of Aaron and Levi could be priests. Bloodline was everything. Of course, Jesus changed all that. Jesus, the supreme Priest, was a descendant of Judah. And when the Holy Spirit fell on the disciples and His new church was born, suddenly the "common person" could be a priest or minister. Everyone in the church; man, woman, slave or free, was equal and God had no problem releasing His spiritual gifts on everyone. The anointing of God now defined who was a priest and a minister, not genealogy.

"But you are a chosen generation, a royal priesthood, a holy nation, His own special people that you may proclaim the praises of Him who called you out of darkness into His marvelous light; who once were not a people but are now the people of God, who had not obtained mercy but now have obtained mercy." (1 Peter 2:9-10)

Peter understands that not only are we all priests, but we who were not united in any way, are now the people of God. Through His mercy, God loves us, and through His Spirit He unites us. And our ministry is to "proclaim the praises of Him who called you out of darkness into His marvelous light."

"You shall eat the riches of nations." Do you remember the story of Jesus and the woman at the well? (John 4) Jesus stopped there because He was too tired to even walk the rest of the way to town. He sat down and sent His disciples ahead. A woman approached, and they started a conversation. He ministered to her, and by the time the disciples returned, Jesus was so "jazzed" about awakening her to the truth of God, that He was no longer tired or hungry. He had "eaten the riches of the nations," led her into a deeper relationship with God, and that had nourished His soul and body. He was reveling in the new-found glory that was hers in God, and it brought Him great joy!

He gave us the great commission to go and do that everywhere (Mark 16:15). Through Him we can "eat of the riches of the nations and revel in their glory" just as He did. We can watch with joy as people receive the Lord and display the glory of God!

> "And I will cut an everlasting covenant for them, and their seed shall be known among the nations, and their offspring among the people; all who see them shall acknowledge them, that they are the seed that Jehovah has blessed." (Isaiah 61:8-9)

Here is Jesus resurrected from the dead; the new, everlasting covenant of life. Everyone who has believed and who believes today has been set apart for the church. We trust in a God who loves us. We put our faith in a God we cannot see, knowing He is greater than any image made by man's hands. Our lives together should be a testimony of His goodness for all the world to see!

> "I will greatly rejoice in Jehovah. My soul shall be joyful in my God. For He has clothed me with garments of salvation; He put on me the robe of righteousness, even

as a bridegroom is adorned with his ornament and a bride with her jewels." (Isaiah 61: 10)

Why should we not rejoice? Jesus has done everything for us: redeemed us, saved us, brought us into everlasting life with the God of love. His robe of righteousness qualifies us to receive from God and enter His presence. No work of ours and no amount of prayer or pious living will get us there. No ritual or event will get us there; only the precious blood Jesus shed for us, our garments of salvation. And these garments, these robes, are so beautiful they are like jewel-encrusted bridal garments, the best God has to offer. And we, when we put them on, understand just how special we are. We *are* the bride of Christ. We will greatly rejoice in Jehovah!

"For as the earth comes out with her buds, and as a garden causes that which is sown to grow, so the Lord Jehovah will make righteousness and praise to grow before all the nations." (Isaiah 61:11)

This is the mystery. We are amazed that a seed planted in the ground, a dead thing, decomposes in the earth, far from our sight, but a living plant emerges weeks later to grow vibrant and green; full of life. We can't understand how all this works, but it is enough to know that God plants us, dead and lifeless, into His presence and from our death He creates life everlasting. Our lives with Him grow our righteousness and praise until no one can deny that God cares for and loves us.

When Jesus stood to read the first verse of Isaiah 61, He was announcing to the world and to the coming church that He is the answer to the earth's tears. He is the One who teaches us how to have full communion with God. He is the One who saves us from death. Through Him and the Holy Spirit the scriptures are revealed. And from Him all blessings flow to us, giving us healing, life, and joy, and setting us apart for all the world to see.

DIGGING DEEPER

- **Read Isaiah 61: 1-3**. What does it mean to be planted as a tree of righteousness? If the church is a "forest," what does it look like when trees of righteousness interact with each other?

- **Read Isaiah 61: 8-9.** Who or what is "the seed" and "the offspring" of the church?

  How are these ministries and people testifying to the glory of God?

- **Read Isaiah 61:11 and Psalm 127:1**
  If God does not build the house, they who build it labor in vain.

  What do these 2 verses have in common?
  What can the church do to "bend into God's construction?"

The church is for the world

"Now may the God of peace who brought up our Lord Jesus from the dead, that great Shepherd of the sheep, through the blood of the everlasting covenant, make you complete in every good work to do His will, working in you what is well pleasing in His sight, through Jesus Christ, to whom be glory forever and ever. Amen." (Hebrews 13:20-21)

God's zeal for His church is unstoppable; powered by a love beyond our comprehension.

Sometimes all we can do is stare at the wonder of it. That it manifests in ways we had not considered is an opportunity for us to grow, not to judge. He is the One who is perfect, and we must strive to be more like Him.

"For Zion's sake, I will not be silent; and for Jerusalem's sake, I will not rest; until her righteousness goes forth as brightness, and her salvation as a burning torch. And nations shall see your righteousness, and all kings your glory. And you shall be called by a new name which the mouth of Jehovah shall name. You also shall be a crown of beauty in the hand of Jehovah, and a royal diadem in the palm of your God. You no longer shall be called Forsaken; nor shall your land any longer be called Desolate. But you shall be called, My Delight is in Her; and your land, Married. For Jehovah delights in you, and your land shall be married. For as a young man marries a virgin, so shall you marry your sons. And as a bridegroom rejoices over the bride,

so your God shall rejoice over you."
(Isaiah 62: 1-5)

This is our God. One who constantly is consumed with our welfare. He will not rest until His people are bright with His holiness that's seen across the world. God is renaming us, changing our DNA if you will, to reflect Him and we will be known as a people who delight God. He makes us a crown and a diadem, unmistakable signs of royal authority and sovereignty.

The world will see the handiwork of God and stop calling God's people forsaken and desolate, but a people God blesses. They shall see the care we take for the next generation and each other and compare it to marriage vows. Our love for future generations shall be tender and exciting like a young man's love for the purity and beauty of his new bride walking up the aisle to meet him. But God will rejoice over us like a bridegroom who sees past the ceremony into the future and understands the joy of a long life lived together in love. Through the years, good and bad, He will rejoice because of the love He has for us and the love we return to Him.

"Hold fast what you have, that no one may take your crown. He who overcomes I will make a pillar in the temple of My God, and he shall go out no more. I will write on him the name of My God and the name of the city of My God, the New Jerusalem, which comes down out of heaven from My God. And I will write on him My new name." (Rev. 3:11-12)

A bride lives under the protection and blessing of the Groom. Just like an earthly marriage, we must work to keep the relationship holy and loving. God is not saying it will be an easy ride. In fact, here in Revelation, He tells us that people will come against us to "take your crown" and that there will be adversity from without and within that we must overcome.

But they who hold fast and overcome will have peace. "Go out" refers to the need to take your army and weapons out of the city to fight an enemy. We, as daughters and sons of God, will unmistakably be known as God's people, protected and loved by Him. We will live in peace, going out no more. Our enemies He will make His enemies, and we will overcome all adversity through Him.

"I have set watchmen on your walls, O Jerusalem. All the day and all the night they shall always not be silent; you who remember Jehovah, do not let a pause be to you. And give no pause to Him until He sets up and makes Jerusalem a praise in the earth." (Isaiah 62:6-7)

God knows that we cannot sustain this life of devotion without help. "I have set watchmen on your walls. . . all the day and all the night they shall always not be silent." There are those in the church who are called to pray. They carry great responsibility. They pray to God all the time for the welfare of His people. They see danger and call to arms. They see sin and call to repentance. They see blessing and call for joy. They call out to God in every circumstance, working for the good of His bride (the church) in the world. These praying men and women are the watchmen of the church.

They pray without immediate reward, sometimes for years before seeing an answer. Their faith is great in a God who loves His church. They know that God will come through, and they are willing to wait for His timing. Relentlessly they pray, never ceasing, never being quiet, until God moves, and their prayers are answered. Then they are given a new charge, and the process starts again.

Do not think this is unrewarded and difficult work. God blesses those who reach for Him. There are personal blessings and growth in this calling that can be found nowhere else in the life of the church. There are blessings of joy when all seems lost. It is a relationship with God that brings life to dormant desires and strength to a struggling faith.

God knows watchmen sometimes bear a heavy burden, but Jesus says--

"Come to Me, all you who labor and are heavy laden,

and I will give you rest. Take My yoke upon you and learn from Me, for I am gentle and lowly in heart, and you will find rest for your souls. For My yoke is easy and My burden is light" (Matthew 11:28-30).

When we pray for the Church it is an opportunity for Jesus to minister to *us* and for us to experience the lightness of His burdens.

"Jehovah has sworn by His right hand, and by the might of His arm; surely I will no longer give your grain as food for your enemies; and the sons of a stranger shall not drink your new wine for which you have labored. But those who have gathered it shall eat it, and praise Jehovah. And they who have collected it shall drink it in My holy courts." (Isaiah 62:8-9)

The tide will turn. God has said it. His people will prosper. The hard times are behind us. We now live under God's mercy and protection.

This is the answer to the watchmen's prayers – salvation! God's own arm will change the future to bless His people. No more will war plague His children, but our labors will bear good fruit. We will remember our hardships and praise God for His deliverance.

This is a promise for the church. So many of us are struggling under the yoke of insider "wars" between members or long-standing members leaving to take their resources to another church. This burden was never ours to bear. Remember, <u>God</u> builds the house. We cannot let ourselves be distracted by what we believe success looks like. Success is not the goal, living the will of God is our ultimate success. When we return to our purpose, to glorify and praise God, He will bless us again with prosperity. When the watchmen pray God's heart back into the church, the tide will turn. God has said it. His people will prosper. The hard times are behind us.

So many churches are struggling today. These "Pollyanna" words seem shallow when you're facing a financial deficit or dwindling membership. This is the battlefield. When our reality doesn't line up with God's promises, we must fight (sometimes that's psychologically) to keep our crown, our identity as sons and daughters of the most Holy Lord. It is our time of walking in blind faith and standing on God's promises.

I pray in a small group dedicated to the spiritual health of our church. Our goal is to usher in His presence for all the congregation and leadership. We pray with the pastor in unity. This church is not without its challenges, and there was a time when our group had dwindled to about 4. The atmosphere of our church was demoralizing; dropping membership through offense and frustration, fear of financial ruin, strife within the staff, all were working toward collapse. We were very discouraged, but we continued to meet and pray.

I remember one week there were only 2 of us at the meeting and we just sat there and looked at each other. Completely overwhelmed, we had no idea how to pray. In fact, we wondered if we should keep on praying at all! But we screwed up our courage and determined not to quit.

Our prayer that day went something like this, *"God, we don't know what to pray. We don't even know Your will for this church. It all seems hopeless and we are tired and depressed. You come into this mess. Only You can fix it. It is beyond anyone's ability. We will keep praying, but You've got to do this."*

His answer was to shore us up, give us the strength and faith to keep going. Time has passed, and we have been faithful, and things are getting exciting! The worship in the service is revitalized, and God is undoubtedly inhabiting our praise. The prayers and teachings of the leadership are moving into empowerment from the goodness of God. People are becoming enthusiastic about a closer relationship with God. There are still challenges, but the whole atmosphere is changing to joy. Go God!

"Lord, I believe; help my unbelief!" (Mark 9:24)

This is the cry of a man who wants Jesus to heal his son. I hear every Christian's voice in that cry. He believes, but he needs more faith for the task to be completed. And Jesus answers his cry with healing, implying that more faith for the father was also given.

Are we not the same?

Ask God for faith to "help me in my unbelief." The Bible is not just inspirational stories. It is a revelation of the nature of our living God, full of teachings we can walk into and live in. God will move in us if we move into Him. God will change our reality if we accept His promises as real.

> "Pass! Pass through the gates; prepare the way of the people! Raise up! Raise up the highway; clear it from stones; lift up a banner over the peoples. Behold, Jehovah has made it heard to the end of the earth. Say to the daughter of Zion, Behold, your salvation comes! Behold, His reward is with Him and His work before His face. And they shall call them, The Holy People, the Redeemed of Jehovah. And to you it shall be called, Sought Out, a city Not Forsaken."
> (Isaiah 62:10-12)

When the world sees the blessing on God's people, they will respond with eagerness. God calls us to prepare the way. We must open the gates of His house to all and clear away all the obstacles and conditions that make it hard for others to come in.

The salvation He offers to the world is Himself given freely, and everyone who accepts Him will be called holy and redeemed. Because the church is guiding people to their salvation, we are called "Sought Out" by the world. Because we know that "we love because He first loved us." (1 John 4:19), we are called "Not Forsaken" by God.

DIGGING DEEPER

- **Read Isaiah 62: 1-3.** If the church is "a crown of beauty in the hand of Jehovah," what does that require of us? How should we function as a church in the world?

- **List 3 blessings watchmen receive.** Why are they important? Who are the "watchmen" in your church?

- "God will move in us if we move into Him. God will change our reality if we accept His promises as real." Think of a promise of God that you claim for yourself. How does your faith in God change your reality to fit His promise?

An intimate look
at a watchman's prayer

"Be faithful and pray as intercessors who are fully alert and giving thanks to God." (Col. 4:2)

Isaiah was God's prophet, yes. But he and his followers were also God's watchmen, intercessors for the nation. This prayer of Isaiah's gives us a close look at how a watchman can be changed and blessed by God just by praying for the people. As we journey through this encounter, we can clearly see how God uses our prayers to bring us into alignment with Himself.

"I will mention the mercies of Jehovah; the praises of Jehovah, according to all that Jehovah has benefitted us, and the great good to the house of Israel by which He benefited them according to His mercies, and according to the multitude of His loving-kindness." (Isaiah 63:7)

"Enter into His gates with thanksgiving, and into His courts with praise. Be thankful to Him and bless His name." (Psalm 100:4)

The protocol for approaching God is to put our cares behind us and remember who He is to us: Redeemer, Savior, Provider, King, One who loves us. . . Isaiah approached the Creator of the universe with respect and humility.

"But they rebelled, and provoked His Holy Spirit, so He was turned to be their enemy; He fought against them. Then His people remembered the days past of Moses, saying, 'Where is He who brought us up from the sea with the shepherd of His flock? Where is He who put His Holy Spirit within him; who led them by Moses' right hand, with His water before them, to make for Him an everlasting name?' (Isaiah 63:10-12)

Judah has sinned, and even though they are not acknowledging this as a nation, Isaiah sees it clearly and confesses on behalf of a callous people. These stories of Moses are not to remind God of His faithfulness, but to build up Isaiah's faith to ask for redemption. Recounting the stories of salvation, Isaiah's confidence is increased as he remembers God's grace and love.

It is essential to focus on God always. We know there are things wrong with the church. We see it every day. But, as watchmen, we must remember the miracles and blessings of God to build our faith. If we do not trust God to work in our community, He will not respond to our request. Building faith is purposeful, a conscious decision to stand on God's promises, to choose God's faithfulness in the face of distress.

"Look down from heaven, and peer from the place of Your holiness and Your glory. Where is Your zeal and Your might? The stirring of Your affections and Your mercies toward me, are they held back? For You are our Father, though Abraham does not know us, and Israel does not acknowledge us; You, Jehovah, are our Father, our Redeemer; Your name is from everlasting." (Isaiah 63:15-16)

Isaiah knows that if Judah does not repent and return to God, things will go badly. He has seen God's place of holiness and glory (Isaiah 6). He has experienced God's zeal and might (Isaiah 42:13). He knows of God's affection and mercy (Isaiah 55:3). He is one of the few in the Old Testament who call God "Father." His intimacy with God was wonderful!

And now He calls on this relationship to save his people. In a Christ-like way, he becomes the intercessor for an entire nation. Their sin may be great, but Isaiah's heart is filled with compassion. Standing alone before God, he claims God's eternal promises for His people. Abraham, the father of the nation, would not recognize his progeny.

Their own brothers, the Jews in Israel, do not look at them. The split between what once was a nation united by a love and devotion to God, has now become so great that Judah and Israel refuse to recognize the other as family. But that doesn't matter. The reality around Isaiah is immaterial. *The facts* are that God is the God of Abraham, Isaac, and Jacob; God is the God of Judah and Israel. Isaiah will stand in the gap for his people and claim all God's promises for them.

> "O Jehovah, why do You make us wander from Your ways? You harden our heart from Your fear. For Your servants' sake, return the tribes of Your inheritance. For a little while Your holy people possessed it. Our enemies have trampled Your sanctuary. We are of old; You never ruled over them. Your name was never called on them."
> (Isaiah 63:17-19)

The glory of God that is so obvious to Isaiah is invisible to the Jews. How can they not see? Isaiah doesn't believe that we, in ourselves, have the power to ignore so great a glory as God's. How could they turn from this glorious God unless He, Himself, had not turned them? How can the God of this people do that?

Isaiah has reached a crisis of faith. This glorious God is in control of the world and the universe. Nothing happens that He doesn't originate. We are not big enough to resist the Creator, so the Creator must have turned our hearts away from Him. Why?

This crisis of faith fuels a cry of deliverance-- *"We are your people, Lord. Our enemies never knew you, but we knew You from of old. You are in our roots and our foundation. You even called us by Your name. Bring us back into Your grace."*

His heart and soul cry out in a fever of compassion and anguish. *"Show your glory, God, and we will return to You."*

"Oh that You would tear the heavens and come down, that mountains would quake before You. As the brushwood fire burns, fire causes water to boil, make known Your name to Your foes, that nations might tremble before You... But we are all as the unclean things, and all our righteousnesses are a filthy cloth. And we all fade as a leaf, and like the wind our iniquities take us away. And there is not one who calls on Your name, who stirs himself up to take hold of You. For You have hidden Your face from us and have melted us away into the hand of our iniquities. (Isiah 64:1-2, 4-7)

There is no deliverance without repentance, and there is no repentance without seeing the love and glory of God and realizing our unworthiness. Therefore Isaiah wants God to rip open the sky and come in glory. He is so great, so beyond our comprehension, that we will be thrown to our knees.

Isaiah acknowledges the nation's sins and unworthiness; the lack of reverence for God by everyone, even to the point of saying, "There is not one who calls on Your name." But this is not giving up on Isaiah's part. Yes, it is true, but God is a God of miracles and mercy. Acknowledging sin is not living in it, but the first step to freeing yourself from it.

This is also God's heart for His people. Isaiah's anguish is what brings this prophecy to us. "O, that You would rend the heavens and come down" is exactly what God did at Jesus' baptism. The heavens opened and the Holy Spirit descended <u>and remained</u>. Seven hundred years after those immortal words were spoken came the answer. Jesus' baptism was the fulfillment of Isaiah's prayer, which became God's word for the world.

"But now Jehovah, You are our Father; we are the clay, and You are our Former; and we all are Your handiwork. Do not be vehemently angry, Jehovah, and do not remember iniquity forever. Behold! Look, please; all of us are Your people. Your holy cities are a wilderness; Zion is a wilderness; Jerusalem is a desolation... Will You restrain Yourself over these things, Jehovah? Will You be silent and surely afflict us? (Isaiah 64:8-11)

Isaiah will not let go of his identity as a child of God. In fact, He uses it to plead his case. "Yes, we have sinned, but we are Your children, the people You formed out of love with Your own hands. And now Your country is in ruins. The jewel of Your nation, Jerusalem, is abandoned. Can You look at this, O God, and not be moved to act?"

All of Isaiah's heartache has been reflecting God's heartache. That His people have rejected Him is a source of anguish for God. He draws out this prayer from Isaiah, this invitation to "rend the heavens and come down" so that He can tell His people that He will do just that. His longing to be with us, to care for us and love us, is not to be denied, and He won't rest until we are safe in His presence. This prayer from Him is our invitation to Him.

Our God of mercy responds with the ultimate sacrifice of love and proof of His promises for us – Himself sacrificed in Jesus. This prayer of intercession is a beautiful glimpse into the depths of God's heart. He tunes Isaiah's heart to His and reveals His love through the prayer that flows from Isaiah. He calls Isaiah to speak the words of repentance so that He can move to heal His people. It is His desire to bring His children into wholeness with Him, and He will give all He has to attain it.

This is the call of the watchman. To tune yourself to God's heart and cry out the prayers God has for His people. Our calling is also our greatest hope.

DIGGING DEEPER

- **Read Isaiah 63: 15-16.** Think of something your church is struggling with. Now spend a few minutes in quiet, asking God for His vision of your church. See past the problem(s) and look for God's hand moving. How has your perspective about your church's struggle changed?

- "The glory of God that is so obvious to Isaiah is invisible to the Jews." Can your church see the glory of God's vision for them? What does Isaiah do to enlighten the Jews? What does God do in answer to Isaiah? How are you benefitting from Isaiah's prayer?

- What do you think your prayer should be for your church? Remember, God loves your church and you must let go of all your offenses to bend into His will.

18

New Heaven and New Earth . . . and a new definition of God's people.

> "But the day of the Lord will come as a thief in the night, in which the heavens will pass away with a great noise, and the elements will melt with fervent heat; both the earth and the works that are in it will be burned up. Therefore, since all these things will be dissolved, what manner of persons ought you to be in holy conduct and godliness. . .?" (2 Peter 3:10-11)

Isaiah has just poured his heart out to God in a prayer of intercession for the Jews. He doesn't yet see the breadth of the whole world redeemed. His understanding of who he's praying for is limited by tradition and teachings of a chosen people separate from unbelievers. This doesn't reflect the depth of God's love for the whole world. God's answer is to expand Isaiah's perception of just who God's people really are.

> "I have been sought, not by those who asked. I have been found, not by those who sought Me. To a nation not calling on My name, I said, Behold Me! Behold Me!" (Isaiah 65:1)

It's like God is saying, "You pray for My people, but you don't know who they are. I call out to the Jews and Gentiles alike and the Gentiles, who never knew Me, answer Me; *they* find Me. They are not even looking for Me and yet they hear Me when I say, 'Behold Me. Here I am.'"

"The people who walked in darkness have seen a great light; those who dwell in the land of the shadow of death, upon them a light has shined." (Isaiah 9:2)

In chapter 9, Isaiah himself proclaimed that the Gentiles will seek and find God, but he still believes this word is only for the Jews. Sometimes our perception of what God is saying hides the truth from us. Will Isaiah grasp it this time? God doesn't give up.

"I have spread out My hands all the day long to a rebellious people who walk in the way not good, after their own thoughts; a people who continually provoke Me to My face, who sacrifice in gardens, and burn incense on the bricks; who set among the graves and lodge in the towers; who eat swine's flesh, and broth of unclean things in their pots" (Isaiah 65:2-4)

God says, "Isaiah, I call to My people to return to Me all day, every day, but they are stubborn, willing themselves not to hear. They go through the rituals they want; not the prayers of faith I gave them. They believe that I am irrelevant, and they choose to worship gods of their own making, believing they can get what they want from them."

The Gentiles are doing the same thing as the Jews, but the Jews are worshipping other gods out of rebellion. The Gentiles are doing it out of ignorance. The softer hearts will hear the true God.

Without thinking, we live the lie that says, "I am more special than they are because I know Jesus, and they do not." Or "My church is one of the few with the truth of scripture. We need to convert them to our way of thinking." Holier-than-thou judgments are not from God, no matter how you wrap them up. They are the things pride makes. God will not honor that. In fact, it is disgusting to Him. He sees the filthiness of the hearts that come to Him insincerely with all the trappings of "holiness" and none of the humility, and it makes Him sick.

"Behold! It is written before Me; I will not be silent, except I repay; yea, I will repay to their bosom, your iniquities and the iniquities of your fathers together, says Jehovah; they that burned incense on the mountains, and have blasphemed Me on the hills. And I will measure their former work on their bosom." (Isaiah 65: 6-7)

This is the state of Israel in Isaiah's day. Isaiah is praying for God to forgive His people and restore them, and God is showing Isaiah just how deep the sin goes, and that sanctifying the Jews will be a very painful process. This is worse than Isaiah thought it was. Now Isaiah is horrified. Is there no hope for Israel and Judah? His heart was breaking for his people, and God seems to have rejected them.

"So says Jehovah: As the new wine is found in the cluster, and one says, do not destroy it for a blessing is in it; so I will do for the sake of My servant, not to destroy the whole. And I will bring forth a seed out of Jacob, and out of Judah one to inherit My mountains. And My chosen one shall inherit, and My servants shall live there." (Isaiah 65:8-9)

Yet here is God with hope in His plan. Isaiah did not understand the import of God's words, but God is proclaiming Jesus' birth and ministry. Jesus is the blessing in the cluster; His new covenant made on the cross is the new wine for us (Luke 22:20). Jesus is the seed out of Judah who, as Son of God, claimed full rights of inheritance from God (Matthew 2:6, Colossians 3:23-24). Jesus freely gives us all of Himself and prepares a house for us in God's presence so we can live there (John 14:2). In His presence is abundance of provision and spiritual peace (Psalm 16:11).

Isaiah did not know Jesus, but he knew these promises of God. His faith grew in the knowledge that what God says He will do – He will do. Hebrews 11, that great chapter on all the men and women of faith throughout time, says, "And all these, having obtained a good testimony through faith, did not receive the promise. . ." (Hebrews 11:39) They rejoiced in faith just to know the promises of God, never seeing them realized in their lifetime. Yet, they lived every day as though they would. This is foolishness to the world, but it is the greatest faith and blessing to God.

Israel and Judah knew God and chose the foolishness of the world.

"But you are those who forsake Jehovah, who forget My holy mountain, who array a table for Fortune and who fill mixed wine for Fate. And I will number you to the sword; and you shall all bow down to the slaughter; because I called, and you did not answer. I spoke, and you did not hear; and you did evil in My eyes; and you chose that in which I had no pleasure. (Isaiah 65: 11-12)

God cannot bless a people who rebel against Him and continue to consult fortune-tellers and tea leaves. In our day the church is so often focused on money or numbers. Programs to increase membership are our idols. "How many people left the service happy" becomes our identity. "How many people attended this week" becomes our success. "How many children were in Sunday School" is our hope for the future.

We stubbornly hang on to these ideas because they are what we choose to define us. God no longer leads His house, but *we are led by what we _think_ God wants*. This is a choice to do that in which God has no pleasure. Churches decline and die because they will not change; they will not let go of traditional thinking. There is no life for those who choose death; there is only death.

Free will is a responsibility that many take lightly, but our eternal lives are at stake. God wants Isaiah to know that there is no grace for stubborn hearts and resistant ears. He needs to let go of the notion that being in the bloodline of Abraham offers guarantees. We also need to let go of who we think God's people are.

God is working to give us a bigger vision of His people.

"So the Lord Jehovah says this: "Behold, My servants shall eat but you shall be hungry. Behold, My

174

servants shall drink, but you shall be thirsty. Behold, My servants shall rejoice, but you shall be ashamed. Behold, My servants shall sing for joy of heart, but you shall cry from heartbreak, and howl from breaking of spirit, and you shall have your name for a curse to My chosen. And the Lord Jehovah shall kill you and He shall call His servants by another name. (Isaiah 65:13-15)

There are children of God we cannot see or imagine. We must set our heart on *all* of His creation, and then we will see children of God in surprising places. We will know His children not by their birth-right or their location, but by His blessings on them. They will be joyful when the rest of the world is depressed. They will be happy in God's presence while others are ashamed. We must look to the hearts of anyone anywhere to see God's people.

I love this phrase, "And the Lord Jehovah shall kill you and He shall call His servants by another name." It sounds so wrathful but isn't it just what baptism is?! Jesus said, "Most assuredly, I say to you, unless one is born again, he cannot see the kingdom of God" (John 3:3).

Paul further develops this in Romans 6---
"our old man was crucified with [Jesus], that the body of sin might be done away with, that we should no longer be slaves of sin. . .For the death that He died, He died to sin once for all, but the life that He lives, He lives to God. Likewise, you also, reckon yourselves to be dead indeed to sin, but alive to God in Christ Jesus our Lord." (Romans 6:6, 10-11)

In other words, here is God's word fulfilled. The Lord Jehovah kills us in our sin through the cross of Jesus Christ and raises us up to a new life and a new name through the resurrection of Jesus. This is not God's wrath against His people, but His solution and deliverance for them to be free of the corruption in this world; the corruption that they lived in through rebellion and ignorance.

We should rejoice that we live in the time of these words! *We* are those children God was talking about to Isaiah. *We* are living in the fulfillment of His prophecy!

> "He who blesses himself in the earth shall bless himself in the God of truth. And he who swears in the earth shall swear by the God of truth; because the former distresses are forgotten; and because they are hidden from My eyes." (Isaiah 65:16)

God says, "See the future, Isaiah. See a time when all people know Me, and I remember their sins no more. A time when everyone is blessed because they understand Me and have a relationship with Me."

We don't know how Isaiah reacted to this news. I don't know how *you* are reacting to this news, but God is about to show us all how He does things.

> "For behold, I create new heavens and new earth. And the things before shall not be recalled, and shall not go up on the heart. However, be glad and rejoice forever in what I create. For, behold, I create Jerusalem a rejoicing and her people a joy. And I will rejoice in Jerusalem, and joy in My people. And the voice of weeping and the voice of crying shall no longer be heard in her. (Isaiah 65: 17-19)

God's not going to fix things, He's going to recreate them! New heavens. New earth. We must open our mind to a new world of joy, peace, and righteousness. Old ways of measuring and understanding are irrelevant. This is a world where His kingdom is manifested and His children, whoever they are, are blessed.

> "For I consider that the sufferings of this present time are not worthy to be compared with the glory which shall

be revealed in us. For the earnest expectation of the creation eagerly waits for the revealing of the sons of God." (Romans 8:18-19)

We must open our church to receive these children of God and put away our ideas of what that looks like. We must open our heart to *become* these children of God and put away our ideas of what <u>that</u> looks like! It's all new. It's something we've never seen before, never imagined before.

Isaiah knew God's heart; he just couldn't see with God's eyes. So, God took him on a spiritual journey of revelation, expanding his mind and his faith to see the grander picture.

We are called to do the same. We must connect with God's heart and allow Him to redefine what the church will look like to us. This can't happen until we accept the journey of faith; we all need to take; a journey that takes us deep within ourselves for healing and deep within God for joy and faith.

DIGGING DEEPER

- Review Isaiah's prayer journey and how he changed in Isaiah 65. Do you see yourself in his journey? In what ways are you like Isaiah?

- "God no longer leads His house, but we are led by what we **think** God wants." We are all vulnerable to this thinking. List a few ways your church has made this mistake. How will you pray for your church now?

- **Read Isaiah 65: 17-19.** List 3 ways God has created "new heavens and new earth" in your life. In your church.

- Now consider that what God has done (even just a minute ago) is no longer new! Are you willing to let go of that understanding and look for something you've never seen before?

Worship as Warfare

"For we do not wrestle against flesh and blood, but against principalities, against powers, against the rulers of the darkness of this age, against spiritual hosts of wickedness in the heavenly places." (Ephesians 6:12)

"For as the new heavens and the new earth which I will make stand before Me, states Jehovah, so shall your seed and your name stand. And it will be from new moon to its new moon, and from sabbath to its sabbath, all flesh shall come to worship before Me, says Jehovah. And they shall go out and see the dead bodies of the men who have transgressed against Me, for their worm shall not die, nor their fire be put out, and they shall be an object of disgust to all flesh." (Isaiah 66:23-24)

Our fight is not with each other. God speaks plainly that He fights our enemies and they are not flesh and blood. When God says that His people will worship Him 24/7 (new moon to new moon and sabbath to sabbath) that means we're not fighting, we're worshipping. And what happens when we do that? Without raising a weapon, we see the dead bodies of our enemies strewn about the ground. This is God's vision of warfare.

When we choose to fight each other, we are left with our own skills and weapons; with our own knowledge of our opponent. Usually, that means we've been offended or hurt and so we decide to hurt them back. We have no discernment that the true enemy, who comes to steal, kill, and destroy (1 John 4:4), is using our emotions against us.

I knew a woman whose husband betrayed her. She never forgave him and, although she cared for him until he died, she was led by her resentment toward him. More than once, I saw her leave him behind as she walked into Church. Her back to him was an unmistakable sign of her anger and hurt. Her attitude was, "It's his fault. I'm a good person just because I'm staying with him. They don't know the hurt I've suffered." Completely lost in her own feelings, her prayers for her husband went unanswered. Could it be God saw her stubborn refusal to forgive tainting her prayers? She should have been fighting against the spiritual forces that were tearing her marriage apart: shame, unforgiveness, anger, . . . Now her husband is dead and it's too late.

There was once another woman who was convinced I had stolen $30,000 from her. It was 2008, and she had lost a portion of her investments during the economic crash at that time. That is a large amount of money, and at the time, I was helping her manage her finances, so I was the logical choice for the charge. Banks were collapsing. The American government poured billions of dollars into Wall Street to keep the country from falling into another great depression. Millions of people lost all their money and their homes. And that's just what happened in America. Nations across the world were facing financial ruin. The world economy was collapsing in on itself. That this woman only lost 10% of her investments should have been cause for celebration, but she did not understand what had happened to the world economy and was sure I had stolen her money. Her stockbroker tried to explain it to her. I tried to explain it to her. She would not listen and brought formal charges against me. I had to hire a lawyer and open all my personal accounts, business accounts, and my tax returns, for investigation.

That was difficult to go through. I felt unjustly attacked and helpless. Although I was innocent, my faith in our justice system is not unshakable, and I wondered what the consequences could be. In my prayers, God clearly said that I should not return a defense (that would mean attacking her). I let the investigation run its course, and I prayed. I prayed against the spiritual forces that were convincing her I was a criminal. I asked for God to intervene on my behalf. I worshipped this God, who wants only the best for me. I focused on the spiritual instead of the natural and continued to love this woman. When my friends learned what was going on, they were outraged, but God had given me peace, and I was not going to move away from it.

After a few months, when no evidence was found, the charges were dropped. She never was convinced I hadn't cheated her, but she stopped telling everyone she could about the situation, and our lives settled down. She lived in turmoil, believing lies and being tormented by her feelings. I accepted God's peace and was able to move on from the situation with forgiveness.

This is not a story about me, but about the power of the Lord to save. He fights for all His children.

During that crash, I was one of the ones who lost everything, my business, my home, half my income. I ended in bankruptcy, and in my fifties had to start building my life over again from nothing. The whole thing brought intense feelings of despair and frustration. But we are not defined by our feelings. We are children of God, defined by His peace, joy, and righteousness. When the world revolts against us, we have a powerful weapon at our disposal that cuts down the enemy at the source.

How do we fight an unseen enemy who can use our very psyche against us? Only through worship. We can't understand it, but God can fight for us. Jesus, our Savior, uses "the exceeding greatness of His power" to fight for us. Since the God who created everything has seated Jesus "far above all principality and power and might and dominion, and every name that is named" (Ephesians 1:21) throughout time (which means even things mankind has made up today), we have the authority that reigns over everyone and everything working on our behalf.

Don't try to understand this; just accept it. Our limited minds cannot understand the totality of what this means, but we can understand that everything and everyone we face in adversity will be conquered by Jesus Christ.

Repeatedly God gives us testimonies of His victories because His people worshipped. Hezekiah prayed and worshipped God and God completely destroyed the Assyrians in one night. (Isaiah 36-37) Jehoshaphat was also given the victory over his enemies without firing a shot. Jehoshaphat assigned worshippers to march in front of Israel's army praising God and *"when they began to sing and to praise, the Lord set ambushes against the"* enemies *of Jehoshaphat and they destroyed one another. (2 Chronicles 20:22-23)*

Paul and Silas were in a dungeon in shackles, waiting for execution. Instead of bemoaning their condition, they began to praise and worship God. The other prisoners were amazed listening to their songs. *"Suddenly there was a great earthquake, so that the foundations of the prison were shaken, and immediately all the doors were opened and everyone's chains were loosed." (Acts 16:25-26)*

What happened next is even more astounding. *All* the prisoners were freed, even though Paul and Silas were the only ones worshipping. I wonder what was going through the other prisoners' minds as they listened. Scripture says they were "transfixed." Miriam-Webster's definition of this word is to "pierce with a sharp implement or weapon."

Hmmmm.

Those other prisoners did not try to escape when their chains dropped off, and the doors opened, even though that was a jail for extreme punishments. They were pierced by God's presence and valued it more than their physical freedom. I would love to have heard the sermon Paul preached at that moment! Not only were they physically freed, but they were also freed in every respect!

And they valued this supernatural freedom more than their lives; choosing to remain in jail facing execution rather than leave and miss the gospel.

These men who were firmly entrapped by the enemy and knew nothing of Jesus were freed because Paul and Silas worshipped. Men who would have lived in the enemy camp now were brought to God's side. I mean, God went right into the heart of the enemy camp and pulled them all out! That is victory! That is the power of God's arm! And that is the effectiveness of our worship and praise!!

Remember the story of my "parking lot battle" between the angels and demons? Nothing happened, no matter what I did, until I threw up my hands and truly worshipped God. God moves through the worship of His people. He responds to our love and adoration with blessing and freedom. The most powerful weapon we have against Satan is the worship of a grateful heart. It unleashes God's resources to save and protect His people, showering blessing on His children and devastation on His enemies.

"You shall have a song as in the night when a holy festival is kept, and gladness of heart as when one goes with a flute, to come into the mountain of the Lord, to the Mighty One of Israel. The Lord will cause His glorious voice to be heard, and show the descent of His arm, with the indignation of His anger and the flame of a devouring fire, with scattering tempest, and hailstones. For through the voice of the Lord Assyria will be beaten down, as He strikes with the rod. And in every place where the staff of punishment passes, which the Lord lays on him, it will be with tambourines and harps." (Isaiah 30:29-32)

A song at a holy festival, gladness of heart with music, tambourines, and harps – this is the music of worship and praise. This is the offering of a grateful heart. And this is the source of the descent of God's arm; an arm that causes destruction for the enemies of God's people. *Every place where His punishment is unleashed, it is done with worship.*

Our Saturday morning prayer group loves to go out into the world and pray. Most of the time other people don't know what we're doing (sometimes even we don't know!), but there's always an atmosphere change.

One day we stopped for a late lunch. It was about three o'clock, and the restaurant was entirely empty except for us. We ordered our food, found a table, and during grace, we asked that God bless this place with prosperity; that His goodness be made manifest in blessing. We sensed an attack on the prosperity of the whole town and gave the situation to God, thanking, and praising Him for His goodness. Then we ate, paying no attention to the tables around us. We talked to each other, stories of God's goodness to each of us, until someone said, "Look!" Suddenly, there was a line waiting to order that went all the way across the restaurant and out the door! That line never shortened for the rest of the time we were there. God's arm was descending on lack and bringing prosperity!

Several weeks later we stopped for lunch again in a different town. The restaurant had very few customers, but this time it was the height of lunch hour. Remembering what had happened before, we prayed the same way for this restaurant, for this town. Now we were watching, and, sure enough, people started coming in and coming in. It was amazing and we couldn't stop praising God for His faithfulness.

Time and time again, He has demonstrated His power in our praise. Miraculous healings, demonic deliverance, atmosphere changes, it's all what we have come to expect because we know He works through praise. Prayer and worship have become *the* focus for us. There is nothing more powerful on earth.

When God tells us that "it will be from new moon to its new moon, and from sabbath to its sabbath, all flesh shall come to worship before Me, says Jehovah. And they shall go out and see the dead bodies of the men who have transgressed against Me," He's saying, "You will worship Me, and I will destroy your enemies. You will emerge from your worship to find them all over the ground, dead forever." His enemies are our enemies. We need not fight from our own limited skill and small understanding. Our weapons are not enough for victory. But God, the infinite, unlimited Creator of all things, will bring <u>Himself</u> to bear on Satan for us and we will emerge in victory.

Worship – the most humbling thing we can do and the most powerful weapon we can give to God to use.

DIGGING DEEPER

- What comes to mind when you consider worship as warfare? Do you believe it? Have you experienced it?

- *"You shall have a song as in the night when a holy festival is kept, and gladness of heart . . ."* (Isaiah 30:29).

  If worship is a weapon, then how does using God's weapons against His enemies make us feel? Why do you think God would operate that way?

- *God, the infinite, unlimited Creator of all things, will bring Himself to bear on Satan for us and we will emerge in victory.*

  What does this tell us about God's love for us?

Yesterday's vision is today's reality the church revealed

"Do you not know that you are the temple of God and that the Spirit of God dwells in you?"
(1 Corinthians 3:16)

Isaiah has travailed for God's people, and God has answered him with a vision of God's people in a new heaven and new earth. It is a vision of such magnitude that Isaiah must tell the world; a prophecy of the very birth of the church.

"So says Jehovah, 'Heaven is My throne, and earth the footstool of My feet. Where then is the house that you build for me? And where then is the place of My rest? And My hand has made all these things, even all these things exist,' declares Jehovah. 'But I will look toward this one, to the afflicted, and the contrite of spirit, even trembling at My word.'" (Isaiah 66: 1-2)

These are incredible words! The Jews built magnificent temples where God was known to dwell.

And here is God saying, "I created all the earth and the universe. Do you really think I will be contained in this box you built for Me?"

No. The Creator of all things is saying that He will find His house in a humble and afflicted heart.

"The hour is coming, and now is, when the true

worshippers will worship the Father in spirit and truth; for the Father is seeking such to worship Him. God is Spirit, and those who worship Him must worship in spirit and in truth." (John 4:23-24)

These words of Jesus were spoken to a Samaritan woman who embraced her life of sin; someone who did not understand the nature of God, who was not of the chosen people. But Jesus shared this with her because He saw through all her sin and into her humble and afflicted heart. He saw that she longed to learn that she was a seeker of love. He showed her that her love was not to be found in men, but in God. These liberating words ushered her to a door of freedom she could see, the open arms of the Father waiting to embrace her searching heart. Her willingness to come to God in truth, just as she was with no pretention, was her entrance to the love she was so desperate for.

This is not the state of our church. We concentrate on being holy and creating beautiful places of inspiration. We spend a lot of money and resources to get the music just right, the lights just right, the pictures and banners just right to inspire the people. But our "sacrifices to God," if not from a humble heart, are not acceptable to our God of love.

"He who kills an ox is as if he struck a man; he who sacrifices a lamb is as if he broke a dog's neck; he who offers a present as if it were swine's blood: he who marks incense as if he blessed an idol. Yea, they have chosen their way, and their soul delights in their abominations. I also will choose their vexations and I will bring their fears to them; because I called, and no one answered. I spoke and they did not hear; for they did the evil in My eyes, and chose that in which I had no pleasure." (Isaiah 66:3-4)

Before people can appreciate God's love, they must face their own lack. God has just revealed to Isaiah that He judges people by what their underlying motives are, not their actions, and Isaiah speaks this truth plainly to the people. "Every sacrifice you offer God is unclean and defiles the temple, because your heart is turned to yourself. Because you choose this; because you don't listen when God speaks, He will expose the deepest parts of your hearts and those fears and anxieties will consume you."

Are we listening? There was no heart in their worship. There was no truth to their actions. God will move His people into a new way of connecting; away from ritual and rules, or we will be consumed by our own blindness and self-centeredness.

Our desire to keep our churches "pure" for God motivates us to pick and choose who we will accept as members and who we will reject. If we persist, God will move His church out of our pretty walls and into the very hearts of those we push away.

"Hear the word of Jehovah, those who tremble at His word. Your brothers who hate you, who drive you out for My name's sake, have said, 'Jehovah is glorified.' But He shall appear in your joy and they shall be ashamed. A roaring sound from the city! A sound from the tempest! It is the sound of Jehovah repaying recompense to His enemies." (Isaiah 66:5-6)

These words of comfort are for those who have stayed faithful and paid a heavy price for it. Falsely accused, they have been thrown out of the temple and ostracized by the community. This is what Jesus suffered for us; total rejection from the people who claimed to have the way to God. And yet, through His sacrifice, we can also leave the city of lies and false rituals, be crucified outside the gates, and reborn into God's glory.

Those rejected ones should be suffering outside of God's presence (the temple), but God will be present with *them*. The joy they receive from God in worship and prayer will shame their accusers. Those who claim to be entitled as God's children will cry out with shame when the sound of God's voice is revealed through the praises of His redeemed people, those of humble spirit who sincerely come to God in love.

Sober words for the church.

- Do we dare to judge the spiritual fitness of others when Jesus tells us "You judge according to the flesh; I judge no one." (John 8:15)

- Are we willing to reject a few "undesirables" for the perceived good of the whole when Jesus said, "What man of you, having a hundred sheep, if he loses one of them, does not leave the ninety-nine in the wilderness, and go after the one which is lost until he finds it? (Luke 15:4)

- Are we willing to take the chance that God will leave us and move His church into the hearts of those we have rejected? "He who rejects Me, and does not receive My words, has that which judges him – the word that I have spoken will judge him in the last day." (John 12:48)

- Are we willing to become enemies of God just to keep our opinions of what the church is? "Bring here those enemies of mine, who did not want me to reign over them, and slay them before me." (Luke 19:27)

Or are we able to trust God and be the ones who reveal God's voice through our praises?

"Rejoice with Jerusalem, and be glad with her, all who love her. Rejoice a rejoicing with her, all who mourn for her; . . .for so says Jehovah: 'Behold, I stretch out peace to her like a river, and glory of nations like an overflowing torrent,. And you shall suck; you shall be carried on the side and be dandled on knees. As a man whom his mother comforts, so I will comfort you. And you shall be comforted in Jerusalem. And you will see, and your heart shall rejoice, and your bones shall flourish like the grass. And the hand of Jehovah shall be known toward His servants, and He shall be indignant with His enemies."

The church is the fulfillment of these words of God. It was born and raised in Jerusalem, being formed in the heart of God for His people. Now we can hear His heart say, "Celebrate the presence of God wherever you are. His power manifested through the church is for everyone. Come and drink the milk of His salvation. Come and learn love with the trust of a child on her father's knee. Learn love like a man who returns to the loving arms of his mother in times of pain. In His presence is fullness of joy and victory over torments."

Are we moving into this kind of ministry? Can we hear God calling us to sacrifice our comfort and plans for the good of the children He brings to us? Are we willing to love this much, to yield to God loving through us? We must claim these promises for ourselves, but more importantly, claim them for others. God's compassion for the world must be ours; no thought of self, but only of Jesus for all.

"For behold, Jehovah will come with fire, and His chariots like the tempest, to return His wrath in fury, and His rebuke in flames of fire. For by fire and by His sword Jehovah will execute judgment with all flesh; and the slain of Jehovah shall be many. Those who sanctify themselves, and purify themselves to the gardens . . . these are cut off together,' says Jehovah." (Isaiah 66:15-17)

These gardens were places of pagan ritual sacrifice. Even children were killed there, and Jews participated in this unholy idol worship, thinking their genealogy protected them from God's anger.

Now Isaiah understands we cannot take our salvation for granted. God will judge everyone; Jew and Gentile, alike. No one will be spared the judgment seat experience. Everyone who worships idols will be cut off from the family, no matter the bloodline.

But God is a loving God, and if we will all be judged, then we *all* have access to His saving grace.

"For I . . .[will] gather all the nations and the tongues; and they shall come and see My glory. And I will set a sign among them, and I will send those who escape from them to the nations . . . to the far away coasts that have not heard My fame nor seen My glory. And they shall declare My glory among the nations. And they shall bring all your brothers out of all nations." (Isaiah 66:18-20a)

This is the birth of the new church. In the second chapter of Acts, all the nations and tongues had gathered in Jerusalem and heard these Galileans speaking in their own languages. They had heard the roar of the Lord in the streets and had come to see what was happening.

This was fantastic enough, but the strength of the Holy Spirit was on Peter when he explained to thousands of people what had just happened. He shared the gospel, and no less than 3000 believed and gave their hearts to the Lord that day. That is the glory of the Lord!

But after a while, this new church came under persecution and "those who escaped" went across the world bringing the gospel to everyone. They declared God's glory and believers sprang up, churches were formed, and the Apostles welcomed them all with joy, counting them fellow members of God's family.

Isaiah sees this church coming, this all-inclusive community of God; where the hearts of men and women define the family. No respecter of persons, the church will be diverse: soldiers, influential, famous, poor, middle class, foreigners, Jews, non-Jews, it doesn't matter, God loves them all. And Israel shall see and return, accepting all of God's children as brothers and sisters.

We seem to forget that the apostles were Jews. They were raised in that faith, and while they were with Jesus, He reinforced the truth of the scriptures and words they knew. Paul, who brought salvation to the Gentile world, was a devoted Jew before he met Christ, a Pharisee among Pharisees. These Jews broke with a tradition that taught that all non-Jews were unclean and shouldn't be spoken to. These apostles began the church with a diversity that is not known today.

"For as the new heavens and the new earth which I will make stand before Me, states Jehovah, so shall your seed and your name stand. And it will be, from new moon to its new moon, and from sabbath to its sabbath, all flesh shall come to worship before Me, says Jehovah." (Isaiah 66:22-23)

God revealed our lives to Isaiah 3000 years ago! The new heavens and new earth usher in God's everlasting kingdom and all believers will stand in that day, thrive in that day, rejoice in that day and every day forever. This is Jesus' gift to us, redemption and grace to live this new life.

Even though he never knew the Lord, everything Isaiah's heart cried for is answered in Jesus. The salvation of God's people and heaven and earth is contained in that one Name. Isaiah never saw Him or experienced Him, but he knew of Him from the revelations God gave him. Now Isaiah's faith cries out to us to believe, to see the glory of God revealed. To experience what he only dreamt of.

God's children will not be lost in their sin, unable to distinguish God's voice from any other and chasing after their own desires. We will see clearly the glory of God and choose life. We will hear clearly what God is saying in every moment.

Listening to God

"He who has an ear, let him hear what the Spirit says to the churches." (Rev. 2:29)

"He who has an ear. . ." How do we get this ear to hear God? Someone once asked me to tell them how God speaks. What do we listen for? My answer is not the list or the process you want to hear. Still your mind and body and wait. Worship Him sincerely and thank Him for all His benefits. Open your mind to accept that God will speak to you in the way *you* need to hear, which will not be the same as me. If you listen for God to speak like He does to me, you will not have success. God speaks in visions, dreams, scriptures, audibly; but he also speaks through random thoughts, surprising feelings, silently in His presence, through other people, . . . He does not limit Himself to a few avenues, so we need to be open to whatever He wants to say in whatever means He says it.

The one common thread in all of this is that God seems to give peace inside His words. If your spirit is unsettled by something you think might be from the Lord, take another look, and ask some advice. Spend more time in prayer, considering it. If there is no peace it is probably not Jesus.

Jesus gave us Holy Spirit to teach us all these things. We have the very essence of God inside us. He will influence and teach us to hear clearly and distinguish God's voice from any other. Ask Him to reveal God's word to you. That's a prayer that makes Him happy!

When we come together as a community to wait on the Lord and hear His voice, it is even more powerful. Miracles happen, chains of oppression are broken, darkness flees. When we hear God, we are challenged to move in faith, to take risks in our lives that build our trust in God. When the church hears God and moves out in faith, the sheer volume of that faith, multiplied among the believers, can move mountains in the world.

There is an organization called Bridge Builders whose purpose is to pray for our country. We call to God to influence the national, state and local governments with His will and protect this country from threats.

A few years ago, there was a hurricane off the east coast that was one of the biggest storms ever recorded. The whole coast was gearing up for the devastation that would surely come when that storm reached landfall. They were holding their collective breath, knowing the aftermath would be awful.

We sought God on this, and He led us to pray that the storm would not turn away to hit someone else. Instead, we prayed, "Like Jesus on the Sea of Galilee, we declare to this storm Peace. Be still." Within 12 hours the storm, still over warm water, began to weaken. By the time it reached the coast, it was a tropical storm and, although there was wind damage and flooding, the damage was in no way as bad as had been predicted. The news media was full of surprise. Storms are supposed to grow stronger over warm water, not dissipate!

Our voices, worshipping and praying together with intercessors around the nation, were heard by God. He changed the weather in miraculous ways in answer to our prayer. This is what we can do together.

The power of the church is the magnified power of God working His will through us. This is the new heaven and new earth. This can be the church glorified by God and glorifying Him.

This man, this prophet Isaiah who sacrificed so much to be the voice of God for his people, was rewarded with this timeless vision of God's church in triumph. Let us claim it for ourselves, for it is us Isaiah is talking about. Let us raise the banner, claim our inheritance from God, and give the church to the world as God intended.

"Those who wait on the Lord shall renew their strength; they shall mount up with wings like eagles, they shall run and not be weary, they shall walk and not faint." (Isaiah 40:31)

Go. Walk your journey into God's heart. Don't be afraid. All God's promises are for His people. Go where He takes you. Go together in the community of faith. There is no darkness He cannot overcome. There is no evil He cannot conquer. There is no heart in repentance He will turn away from. There is not one of

His children He will not protect. His church is His bride and He will support us as we seek Him. The way is challenging, but not treacherous, and the end is glorious!

"For I know the thoughts that I think toward you, says the Lord, thoughts of peace and not of evil, to give you a future and a hope. Then you will call upon Me and go and pray to Me, and I will listen to you. And you will seek Me and find Me, when you search for Me with all your heart," (Jeremiah 29:11-13)

"But now, thus says the Lord, who created you, O Jacob, and He who formed you, O Israel. Fear not, for I have redeemed you; I have called you by your name; You are Mine. When you pass through the waters, I will be with you; and through the rivers, they shall not overflow you. When you walk through the fire, you shall not be burned, nor shall the flame scorch you. For I am the Lord your God, the Holy One of Israel, your Savior." (Isaiah 43:1-3)

To Him be the glory forever!

DIGGING DEEPER

- **Read John 4: 23-24.** "God is Spirit and those who worship Him must worship in spirit and in truth." Why does God require such a thing?

- Is there heart in your church's worship? Is there truth in your church's actions? How do you think you should pray for your church?

- **Read Isaiah 66: 18-20a.** "But God is a loving God, and if we will all be judged, then we all have access to His saving grace." What do the scripture and this quote have in common? What is God's calling on His church? On your life?

- **Read Isaiah 43:1-3.** Knowing that all God's promises are for all His people, no matter when they live; what do these verses tell you about your relationship with God? Can you claim this promise for yourself? For your church?

- Take 15 minutes and just praise and worship God. Claim His promises for yourself and catch His vision for you and your church.

TO CONTACT THE AUTHOR

Joy Simons may be contacted via her email:
joynoel57@gmail.com

She can also be followed using her blog:
www.psalm42-7.net

Books may be purchased through the author directly,
Glorybound publishing at
www.gloryboundpublishing.com
or amazon.com

ABOUT THE AUTHOR

Joy is from Hampton, Virginia. She grew up the youngest child of a family of five. Her father was the Director of Music at the First United Methodist Church in a historical building over 200 years old. She has fond memories of her father tickling the keys of the pipe organ. She continued in his footsteps gaining a love for music. It has become her life. She has a Batcher of Music Education from James Madison Univ. and a Master of Music from Northern Arizona University. Through the sands of time she has directed more choirs than she can remember. She has been studying, teaching, preaching and singing about God since she started walking.

Joy has been interested in Isaiah for many years releasing a comprehensive commentary on her personal blog After some time blogging, she realized God wanted her to compile it into a book. It is with honor we now share the intimate intertwined story of *Isaiah and Me*.

Made in the USA
Middletown, DE
17 April 2021